FOUR STAGES
OF
GREEK THOUGHT

The Harry Camp Lectures at
Stanford University
1965

FOUR STAGES
OF
GREEK THOUGHT

JOHN H. FINLEY, JR.

STANFORD UNIVERSITY PRESS
STANFORD CALIFORNIA

Stanford University Press
Stanford, California
© 1966 by the Board of Trustees of the
Leland Stanford Junior University
Printed in the United States of America
Cloth ISBN 0-8047-0274-8
Paper ISBN 0-8047-0275-6
Original edition 1966
Last figure below indicates year of this printing:
87 86 85 84 83 82 81 80 79 78

The Harry Camp Lectures

*The Harry Camp Memorial Fund
was established in 1959 to make possible
a continuing series of lectures
at Stanford University on topics
bearing on the dignity and worth
of the human individual.*

PREFACE

The first three of these lectures were delivered in early 1965 in what to an eastern memory remains the Phaeacia of Stanford. "There high trees grow blooming," said Homer. "Their fruits never wither nor fail, winter or summer, the year around, but the blowing west wind continually hatches some and ripens others." The fourth lecture was added later. If apology is desirable for treating great subjects in a small space, it is wholeheartedly offered. Since innumerable pages cannot in any case recapture the Greek enchantment, one recourse seems simply to contemplate it. The notes are largely to passages cited; to have tried for reasonable completeness would have been to multiply them indefinitely. Memory of the charm and hospitality of friends in Stanford remains Phaeacian too—above all, of the incomparable company of Philip and Virginia Rhinelander.

J. H. F.

Cambridge, Massachusetts
December 1, 1965

CONTENTS

Chapter One

THE HEROIC MIND

"This human mind," Emerson said, "wrote history, and this must read it. . . . There is a relation between the hours of our life and the centuries of time." On first impulse one agrees. Ancient words wake recognition that can seem from yesterday, and if the setting differs, we feel more strongly the persistence that can thus overarch change. Yet a little thought gives pause. How, exactly, are we to conceive this survival? From Vico, through Brooks Adams, to Spengler and Toynbee, some have thought the reason political: the body politic, like the human body, they think, lives its cycle, and we recognize in past civilizations stages that we know in our own. But granted that situations recur—for example, that nations, like people, are freer to sketch and plan when institutions have yet to be built and resources are still uncommitted than at a later stage when the die has been cast and one must live with what one has chosen—granted this and much else, the notion of a life-span of civilizations remains troublesome. History is a road with countless forks; to go down one turn of the fork is to renounce the landscapes that might have opened to the other, and when this act of choice and exclusion has recurred innumerable times, who can say that any path will be retraced? These lectures will reflect no such view but the outlook, rather, of an older and less elaborate classicism. Writers of just before and after the Christian era—notably Horace, Longinus, and Quintilian—first fully expressed the notion that past works fall into classes, hence that the chief works of any class best exemplify it, hence that these works serve an illustrative function.[1] A classic is thus an exemplar—but an exemplar of what? Here one is back with Emerson, and can only say that, fresh as the future surely is and unknown as is the terrain that awaits, yet other travelers have seen things and, since people are interested in each other and all travel has certain constants, these past reports are relevant, and the greater and more inclusive, the more relevant. Whether the Greeks saw things most freshly because they came first or it is pure good luck that, having come first, they answered life with unmatched alertness, they in either case keep ageless sparkle, as of the world lit by a kind of six-o'clock-in-the-morning light and the dew imperishably on the grass. The Greek mind remains in ours, because this untarnished freshness leaves it, like youth itself, our first exemplar.

We shall pursue four stages of it, each evoked by new conditions, as it summoned new powers to survey an altered scene. The later stages were obviously conditioned by the earlier. One never sees successive reality with quite fresh eyes, but partly through habit and association; yet novelty does appear, and the mind somehow advances into it, apparently much as stones in an arch, though partly resting on the ones below, yet partly reach out into empty space. Few things are more moving than this reaching into the unknown. The act itself may be the supreme past exemplar, and since we both resemble and differ from anyone before us, the sight of others coping with novelty gives assurance of our power to do so. Moreover, we may profit from their steps, not, to repeat, because we shall ever meet anything exactly similar but because clarification of even a part of the mysterious unknown gives confidence. I am still reverting, I fear, to the idea of exemplar. One would surely reject the classic if it meant that all problems were solved and all norms established. It obviously does not mean that; yet inheritance does mean, as it meant for successive stages of antiquity, that certain things may be securely accepted as admirable. The problem then becomes one of reconciling regard for the received with growth into the unknown. The true classic at once gives and spurs, and it can do both simultaneously because in the immensity and novelty of experience sharing is not hostile to independence—on the contrary, is the self's first companion and longest interlocutor.

Our first stage is Homer, but though the title "The Heroic Mind" is appropriate, it may not quite fit what will follow. I am interested rather in an outgazing bent of mind that sees things exactly, each for itself, and seems innocent of the idea that thought discerps and colors reality. One is right in judging such a mind natively heroic; it has no doubt that what it sees is real, acts abruptly on that unquestioned assumption, takes the consequences of its actions, lives with imperatives that, so to speak, reside in things themselves because they are inherently noble and beautiful, not because we think them so.

When in the sixth book of the *Iliad*[2] Hector briefly returns to Troy from the battlefield and in a famous scene meets his wife and infant son at the gate and reaches out to take the boy in his arms, the child draws back frightened at his father's bronze armor and helmet with horsehair crest; whereupon Hector laughs, takes off the helmet, and lays it all-shining on the ground. In so deeply felt a scene surely no one but Homer would have paused to note that helmet still shining beside the human figures. It is as if in whatever circumstances it too keeps its particular being, which does not change because people are sad or happy but remains what it is, one of the innumerable fixed entities that comprise the world. Similarly in the heroic poems ships remain swift, bronze sharp, the sky starry, rivers eddying. Though heroes fight and die, everything in the outflung world keeps its fit and native character. Again, in the seventeenth book of the *Odyssey*[3] when Odysseus, still in the guise of a beggar, at last first approaches his house and the dog Argus, left behind twenty years before and now old and neglected, sees his master, lowers his ears, wags his tail, but lacks strength to move, does Odysseus commiserate with him or pat him? On the contrary, after secretly wiping away a tear, he says to his companion the swineherd, "What a handsome dog there on the dung-heap! But was he fast in the chase or simply a table-dog?" And the swineherd gives the expected answer, "That is the dog that Odysseus left behind when he went to Troy, and none was faster or braver to track down beasts in the depths of the thick woods." Odysseus enters the house, and the dog dies, the first to have recognized him at home. He had for a dog the virtue that

Hector's helmet had for a helmet. Each, like all the other people and objects in the poems, keeps its inherent nature, and a chief marvel of the poems might be said to be the ineffable act of concentration whereby men and women, great people, small people, towns, fields, animals, seas, rivers, earth, sky, and the lucent gods themselves, remain each distinct while jointly comprising the brilliant world.

How conceive the working of such a mind? Theoretical answers, though hardly complete, go a certain distance, and chief among them, it scarcely needs be said, is the work of the Californian Milman Parry, who died at thirty-three in 1935 after revolutionizing Homeric studies.[4] Apparently as early as when he first read Homer in college, he thought him so unlike other poets that he must have composed in some unusual way. This different way, Parry came to think, was the so-called oral method of composition which he spent his short life elaborating, partly by theory, partly by learning Serbian and coming to know at first hand the oral poetry of Jugoslavia. Briefly put, this theory of oral composition postulates two main conditions: first, a body of legend about bygone heroes whose feats gathered about a few famous enterprises; second, and more crucial, a body of language passed from generation to generation but freshly used and slightly changed by each age and singer that enabled singers to compose complete verses as they went along. The familiar Homeric line introducing a speech may illustrate in small the complex process: "Him answering addressed swift-footed Achilles." The line falls into halves: Achilles at the end, how he spoke at the start. Now Parry noted that any other character, if provided with a suitable epithet, might metrically replace Achilles at the end of the line, a character with a long name like Agamemnon being joined with a short epithet, a character with a short name like Zeus with a long epithet. Similarly at the start of the line "answering" was not the only stance in which a character might speak; he might do so "standing up," "with a scowl," "with good intent," "fainting," or in a number of other ways that—and this is the important point—are metrically equivalent to "answering." Taken together, the options at the end and at the start of the line give the singer a set of choices by which he may introduce any character speaking in some fitting way. One may not call such a line memorized in the usual sense of the word; rather, it is composed from memorized elements, proves metrical because these elements were so intended, suits all the characters and many kinds of situations because its terms had been perfected for that purpose—in short, lets the singer simultaneously advance his story and compose a verse.

Needless to say, this simple example does small justice to the subtle tradition that supplied a singer with fit and metrical words in the quick moment when he needed them, supplied him too with procedures and motifs for describing battles and banquets and messages and a thousand such recurrent events, supplied him even with the tone and cast of a gallery of characters. The extraordinary fact that one must keep recalling is that through the centuries when the art was elaborated no one ever read a poem or had in fact learned anything by reading; in everyone's mind, singer and listener alike, lay the words of the poetic tradition that he had known since childhood and that alone lifted above the small present its arc of completer relevance and meaning. If everyone in a part of his being thought in this greater language and even Achilles in the *Iliad* is pictured as solacing himself by singing, some people by special gifts lived themselves more fully into it, each necessarily in his own way, since, though the language was traditional, it was not fixed in books but had to be recreated by each man, inevitably with the changes that time and temperament dictated. How the Homeric poems came to be written down when the very nature of the art implies the lack of writing is another kind of question, fixed in circumstance and doubtless lost beyond recall. Homer lived in Ionia—so much ancient tradition and his language make clear—in the late eighth century, it is thought, when writing was first emerging beside the oral art.[5] Was he recognized as so great that professional singers, perhaps of his own family, wanted his songs as heirloom of their guild, and did some clever young man—a grandson, one would like to think—see how writing could serve the purpose? If one can only guess in such matters, the oral character of the poems is beyond guess, and it is this that brings us back to the crystalline Homeric world of Hector's helmet and the dog Argus. The helmet shines and the dog was swift, partly because Homer's epithets, that functional element of his oral style, declared them such. Similarly all the other characters and objects of the poems keep identities that the very nature of oral verse-making compelled them to keep. Had Homer conceived the thought of substituting new words and epithets for the received, he would in that act have become a literary poet, and the clear world of his recurrent shapes would have vanished.

Yet that world stayed fixed and clear not only by reason of the oral style, but because Homer and presumably his audience as well thought and wanted it such. The legendary figures of Troy and Mycenae, Ithaca and Pylos, lived on untouched by the thought that they were only thoughts. Hence we return to more elusive questions: what is implied by this unfaltering confidence in outer reality, and why has it so deep a grip on us? It may be said of literary styles that the more elaborate their structures, the more these reflect a man's conscious and ordering thought, and, by the same token, the less they reflect external objects. Thought proceeds by scheme and sequence; it manipulates, puts things where it wants them, makes different designs from any that the eyes see, and, what is more, knows that it is doing so. Conscious art selects from nature and by selecting adds. In the process the forms of nature inevitably take second place; their edges are blunted to fit the ruling design, and the complex final effect, being composed of many parts, diminishes the being of any one part. Yet the price of this triumph is violation of our senses. We evidently see at any moment a sequence of sharp particulars—light at a window, a tree trunk, the gray of a rock—single, peremptory impressions, moving in endless specificity across our vision. A part of our life belongs to them; we know the world and feel at home in it not least through these sure reminders. Happiness, one sometimes thinks, is clarity of vision, moments when things stand clear in sharpest outline, undimmed by familiarity as if revealed for the first time. Such moments bring back, so to speak, the memory of Eden sparkling on the first day of creation, the tree of life soaring in the middle, and if Eden be related to our childhood, they bring back childhood too. In this spirit Gladstone entitled his book on Homer *Juventus Mundi,* the world's youth—evidently not because the *Iliad* is comforting but because it is clear. Literary history abounds in reactions against elaborate and mental styles—for example, in recent times that of Hemingway against, say, Henry James. I remember from an otherwise forgotten story of Hemingway a sentence about a bare light bulb glaring in a diner; the sentence was complete; one saw just that. No more than Hector's shining helmet did the light bulb announce a happy ending, yet it was to this extent happy and confident: it signified impressions that one could trust. However intoxicating the attractions of intellect and however essential to the structures by which we live, something in us wants also the clear signals of the senses by which alone the world is made fresh and definite.

Now, needless to say, words and thoughts, being products of our minds, cannot capture reality, which remains beyond us, an object of faith, not of knowledge. Presumably no leaf or blade of grass or person or object exactly resembles another, but being unable to comprehend a world of unutterable and endless differences, we, as Aristotle said, put things into classes, and keep our sanity by speaking of oak tree or maple tree, man or woman, Frenchman or Englishman—just as if one of these quite resembled another. Hence it cannot be said that in Homer or Hemingway the object described indeed exists or that it quite corresponds to anything that we know. It only carries through a kind of faith the color of reality, and, since we know that we exist and do see and touch things, it evokes the particularity that these things have. But mark what Homer's confidence, by being so complete, also effects. It somehow frees the inner mind, precisely because external objects are so firm, to follow as firmly its imaginative life. The figure of the blind Homer, though conceivably justified by fact,[6] has the higher rightness of showing him peering with inner eyes toward a real but distant past. As early religious painters dressed the shepherds and wisemen of the Nativity in clothes that they themselves knew and by so doing made the miraculous event more present, so because he sees past reality exactly Homer is free to dwell in it as his sense of truth commands. His is not the search for historical truth which costs so much in detail that it exhausts itself before reaching the whole. One sees here his difference from a realism which, wanting a world as firm as his, ends by overweighting the world and letting it cramp the mind's free play. A curious interworking seems to exist between definiteness and freedom. Have we not all known people who, quite sure of their worlds and of what they should and will do, remain at the same time strangely resilient to other people and new situations? They, to be sure, differ radically from those who cling to definiteness as to a lifeline and want stability at all cost. Part of what is so affecting in Homer and, old as the familiar bust imagines him to be, gives him the quality of unfading youth is that sure acceptance of things which lets him see them whole and together. The paradox fol-

lows that heroism of mind is not merely or chiefly concerned
with heroes but sees them only as the summit of a firm brightness that it beholds everywhere.

This brings us to his subject, which is obviously two subjects: Achilles and Odysseus. Some people, to be sure, think
the *Odyssey* not Homer's, and this is not the place to try to
defend the classic view. Briefly, if, as Parry held, an oral style
changes in minor but important and recognizable ways from
singer to singer and place to place, it is hard to believe that
the *Odyssey* could be as close as it is to the *Iliad* in style and
method if it had been composed by a man fifty years younger
who had formed his own habits of singing. We shall assume
a single author but need not think that he composed the two
poems at the same time of life. The ancient critic Longinus
compared the *Iliad* to the sun at noon, the *Odyssey* to the setting sun, of brighter colors but less burning.[7] The comparison
sounds like a reply to ancient opponents of the common au-
thorship, and its language is the happier because much in the
Odyssey suggests that it is an old man's poem. Its analogue
is Shakespeare's *Tempest*: as that radiant play finds a new
world on the other side of ruin and tragedy—a world shared,
so to speak, between the old Prospero on one side and the
young lovers and the beauty of nature on the other—so does
the *Odyssey*. The battered Odysseus has sympathy for old
people who have endured as much as he—the swineherd Eu-
maeus and the nurse Eurycleia—but the young Telemachus
and Nausicaa give freshest renewal, and the green islands of
his travels confirm nature's persisting youth. This is not to
say that in either the *Tempest* or the *Odyssey* the world has

changed; Prospero was nearly murdered on the island and may be again on the way home, and the complacent suitors in Ithaca breathe the tedium of untraveled and unquestioning middle life. It is the old and the young who jointly effect the marvel of life made new, and as if Homer were conscious of the transformation and in some part saw himself now in Odysseus, he several times likens Odysseus to a singer[8]—also gives him notable sympathy with singers[9]—evidently seeing in the traveler who reached home a mood of assent and attainment that he understood. The *Iliad* by contrast shows the secure world in flames and its only survival the incandescent memory of heroes. It is a young man's poem or at least turns on a young man, and Achilles' intransigent hopes, which life does not confirm, end by standing clear above life, kept only by poetry as its treasure and meaning. The *Iliad* sees life from the inside as suffering, the *Odyssey* from the outside as memory, and these differing tones seem the tones of Homer's changing years.

The shining specificity of the oral style unfolds a world that is the fit home of Achilles' youthful hopes. Though at first glance our own childhood memories of the radiant Greek mythology seem disillusioned in the carnage of the *Iliad,* they are not destroyed but, so to speak, put at one remove. At the beginning of the thirteenth book Poseidon crosses the sea to Troy from his familiar haunt at Aegae, with golden chariot and leaping horses, while the waves part and the sea creatures gambol in pleasure at the presence of their lord. The gods that passionately watch and even sway the flow of battle keep their pristine beauty, which in the similes refracts in the brief sight of waves, fields, rushing rivers, and proud animals, and in the epithets recurs in the shadowy mountains and the rosy fingers of the dawn. In the middle of the poem, after Achilles' first disillusionment and withdrawal, old Nestor recalls an embassy ten years ago before the war when, in his father's house, Achilles learned of the great expedition and pressed to join it.[10] One may wonder why the Greeks constructed about Troy rather than about some other Mycenaean enterprise this elaborate record of deeds and people and of the numberless places that they went to or came from. Part of the reason must be that Troy became in later imagination the place of the unknown and of testing. Those that stayed at home—for example, Penelope's suitors and Aegisthus, who courted Agamemnon's wife in his absence and killed him on his return—remained the untested ones, parochial and bounded creatures whose minds had not risen to the width of things. If one imagines Homer as a boy first hearing the heroic songs and later himself singing in Ionian towns, the width to which the heroes responded must have been a width that he felt;[11] this poetry was itself a kind of cliff or headland which alone gave on history and time and the lives and fates of men. "To give to airy nothings a local habitation and a name," says Shakespeare of poetry, and to the Greeks this name was Troy, except that they surely thought it real and, as said earlier, never conceived, at least at this stage, that its chief reality was in their thoughts. Achilles then was only the chief of those who rose ardently to the testing and the unknown, and since this response is from youth itself, he remains the imperishably young.

That he was also, though of mortal father, the child of the sea-goddess Thetis further describes him. His friend Patroclus, of easier nature and readier to abate personal expectations in favor of the general good, later calls his intransigence born of the cruel sea,[12] and something unnegotiable, solitary, unusable in him confirms the statement. If, as Aristotle thought,[13] the *Iliad* is the prototype of tragedies, the tragic hero may be such partly through this intractable and lonely sea-nature. Hector, in a thousand ways Achilles' foil and contrast as well as his adversary in the poem, has nearly every usable virtue. He is a man of duty and society and appears in the setting of father, mother, wife, child, army, and comrades; even in thinking of his death he imagines his tomb and memory surrounded by public honor as by a kind of companionship;[14] yet he is less intense than Achilles and of mortal parentage. Achilles' half-parentage from the sea thus seems to convey not only intransigence but a looking outward toward something vast, impersonal, unconfined by use and presentness, existent in itself. If these traits seem antithetical —the one fiercely aware of what is owed the self, the other dissolving the self in allegiance to something greater—the combination seems characteristic of great natures. Achilles then not only in initial ardor expresses a meaning of the expedition as a leap into the unknown but in his vision of a godlike glory to be won at Troy shows his allegiance to a still greater unknown, which is in himself and guarded by his self-fidelity. The sight of him in the first book,[15] just after his quarrel with Agamemnon, alone by the strand of the resound-

ing sea conveys both loneliness and listening, the mind's isolation, yet affinity with a space beyond itself.

The line that recurs at many deaths in the *Iliad*—he fell
and "darkness veiled his eyes"—can seem the saddest line,
and finally a kind of hallmark, of the poem. The leap
into the unknown on which fame and fortune depend and
which greatness asks does not often end happily. Some make
the leap but in a half-practical spirit, trusting that they will
get home alive and with some profit. In a moment of Agamemnon's discouragement, Odysseus rebukes him, saying of
himself and others: "We are of the breed who have been
taught from youth to age to wind the skein of bitter war until death destroys us."[16] That is not an inconsiderable courage,
somewhat in Housman's Roman spirit, which knows what it
is doing and is willing to take the chance. But few in the *Iliad*
are as conscious as Odysseus of why they are at Troy, and
death is a recurrent surprise. One need hardly rehearse the
story of Achilles' shock and anger when Agamemnon in a
test of authority takes away his captive, the girl Briseis, who
means something to him but who also signifies the regard
that he thinks due his accomplishment. He therefore with-
draws from battle and refuses to return, though Trojan suc-
cesses push the Achaeans nearly into the sea. Only when his
friend Patroclus feels the army's plight does Achilles let him
wear his own armor and lead out his troops, the famous
Myrmidons, though with the warning that he not press his
advantage or pursue the Trojans to the walls.[17] But in his success Patroclus forgets the warning. He meets Hector and is

killed—much as Achilles would one day be killed by Paris
beneath the walls[18]—and he leaves Achilles to grief and self-
reproach. Of the many themes of the poem few are more
mysterious than that of the choice offered Achilles between
a short and glorious and a long inglorious life.[19] Having been
told him, he says, by his mother the sea-nymph, it seems to
convey the uneasy union between her divine nature and the
mortal nature of his father Peleus, as if the safe land could
never keep the sparkling sea. It in any case expresses the ageless knowledge that brightest things are briefest. When Agamemnon's insult had seemed to rob the expedition of its nobility and even of common justice, he had first thought of
returning home to at least a long life, yet had in fact stayed
through some half-understood motive of commitment and
loyalty to friends, and now in Patroclus's death finds the decision made. The short and glorious life that will be his comes
to him, so to speak, as third choice. The first choice would
have been to live gloriously like a god, forever young; the
second to live to an honorable old age surrounded by esteem
in a world that recognizes merit; the actual choice emerges
like a thief from error and disillusion, yet is all that is given.
The goddess Hera, not as giving a gift but as acknowledging
a fact, says that Achilles will be invincible for a day,[20] as he
proves to be in killing countless Trojans and finally Hector.
Natural elements even gather around him as he combats the
rivers Simois and Scamander, source of the former fertility
of Troy, and is supported by the fire of Hephaestus, portent
of the ruin that awaits Troy. His overwhelming but brief triumph and the glory that fame will celebrate are not the tri-

umph and the fame that reflect any comprehensible scheme of things. They are as short as youth itself and both personify and end it. When at the end, in spite of all his grief and of the death that he now knows soon awaits him, he gives Hector's body back to the old Priam, he seems to rest on the ruin of his first bright hopes, instructed, aware of his humanity and of the gods' laws for mankind, but no longer the visionary youth that he was. The end of the poem is the end of youth, and only its incandescence will remain in the keeping of the Muses.

That phrase, the keeping of the Muses, is meant almost literally. Divisionists have been particularly unfeeling toward the scene at the end of the *Odyssey* in which the ghosts of the suitors are guided to the underworld; it is one of Homer's finest. Among the many who watch their arrival are the mighty shades of Agamemnon and Achilles. They are still discussing Troy, and Achilles, now reconciled with Agamemnon, praises him as beloved of Zeus because he ruled at Troy over many and valiant followers. Yet he ends with characteristic bluntness by saying that the king's honor would have been complete had he died gloriously there; as it was, he perished pitifully at the hands of his wife. "But when you were killed," replies Agamemnon, "we fought for your body all day long, and when we retrieved you and brought you to the ships and washed you, a marvel took place: there was a roaring of the sea, at which we were terrified until your mother issued with her sea-nymphs, who lamented you and dressed you in immortal clothing, and with the nine Muses who sang over you."[21] After describing at length his great pyre and burial in a common grave with Patroclus, he concludes, "Thus not even in death did you lose celebrity; forever among all men will your great fame endure, Achilles. But where for me is this regard, after I wound the skein of war? At my return Zeus devised grim ruin for me at the hands of Aegisthus and my baleful wife."[22] After this interchange they notice the ghosts of the suitors; and when Agamemnon asks them who they are and is told, he breaks into passionate praise of Odysseus: felicitous man, he got in Penelope a prudent and faithful wife, report of whose merit will never die but will be fashioned by immortals into song for earthly men.[23] Here at the end of the poem Penelope shares the honor that Odysseus has had throughout it, and husband and wife emerge together as the fit and joint theme of poetry.

Now two of the most gifted recent writers on Homer, Schadewaldt and Whitman,[24] emphasize in ways that may be omitted here the degree to which both the *Iliad* and the *Odyssey* are composed with a sense of the whole Trojan tradition; they illuminate it, sum it up, complete it. If so, this nearly final scene of the *Odyssey* gives something like the ultimate judgment. Of the three greatest figures, one, Agamemnon, though a king on earth and the most powerful of known men, is effectively eliminated; he died miserably, and if his death did not fit his life, it bears on and relates to it. The two remaining figures, Achilles and Odysseus—or in the latter case, the paired figures of Odysseus and Penelope—contain the sum and meaning. Of Odysseus, more in a moment by way of conclusion; of Achilles, he is in the keeping of the Muses. So Pindar later thought in a noble poem on the mingled ruin and grandeur of the Persian war;[25] Achilles remained to him the example of those who had died, and then as formerly the Muses alone give comment. His fame approached him, so to speak, not from the front with foreseen and calculable invitation, but unexpectedly, out of disillusion, anger, and self-reproach. Yet he remains described by the first brightness of expectation that took him to the unknown of Troy, and by his affinity with the measureless sea that shines beyond the fixed and bounded present. The *Iliad,* like all tragedies but seemingly more clearly than any other, is at one and the same time paradoxically very dark and very bright: dark in the actual unfulfillment of what might have been expected and seemed possible, bright in the ardor of that expectation and its persistence over change. Hector's shining helmet and all the other clear and beautiful objects that comprise the visible flash of the world fit and solicit the ardor of this response.

Finally, to turn to Odysseus, the sea that partly describes Achilles obviously describes him too—it is his teacher and he its aptest pupil—but in a somewhat different way. Hector in the *Iliad* is a figure of the land, and the water that identifies him is the benign flow of streams and springs; in his last flight from Achilles, he runs beside the hot and cold springs where the wives and daughters of the Trojans had washed their shining clothes "in peacetime before the sons of the Achaeans came."[26] Land and springs comprise an idyl of peace. Achilles in the *Iliad* is associated also with fire—the fire both of glory and of ruin—and his destruction of Hector and by implication of Troy suggests the lightning stroke that destroys the benign but impermanent house. The house is human; the lightning half-divine. These elements recur with changed suggestion in the *Odyssey*. One never quite knows whether Odysseus likes or dislikes his travels; we first see him on a headland of Calypso's island willing to die if he may only see the smoke upleaping from his rooftop at home; wrecked later at sea, he wishes that he might have died at Troy.[27] Yet his insatiable curiosity keeps him in the Cyclops's cave when his companions want to leave, and he has to be reminded that he has stayed a year with Circe.[28] He is marked by the sea, which makes him the great man that he is, yet in his humanity he renounces it for home. Two episodes describe his choice and its result. The first is when Calypso, justly claiming to be more beautiful than Penelope, offers him agelessness and immortality if he will stay with her; though aware of her divine beauty, he refuses.[29] A famous description had recounted the island's ravishing freshness;[30] in renouncing it, he gives up the eternity of nature—as it were, of untracked beaches and blue water forever flowing in and out of caves— in favor of his mortal identity at home. The second episode is the prophecy of the seer Teiresias in the underworld. Odysseus will indeed reach home, says the seer, but then must take an oar on his shoulder and seek a land where men are ignorant of salt and where a passerby, spying the oar, will call it a winnowing fan; he must then build an altar and sacrifice to Poseidon; returning home, he will rule in peace over a happy people and reach a shining old age, and a gentle death will come to him from the sea.[31] Odysseus is like a runner who cannot stop at once on finishing a race; he must exorcise and placate some restlessness of the sea that survives in him; even when he does so and has pacified Poseidon, something of the sea will return in his death. This wonderful prophecy declares him the reconciler of two worlds; he does achieve home and is profoundly grateful to have done so, yet he would know its virtues less fully than he does—would miss its wonder—if travel had not taught him. He ends, if one may put it so, by crossing to the other side of the measureless sea of Achilles' youth, and the land that he finds is different from Hector's land, because return is different from never having gone away, and attainment different from keeping. In like spirit, the former destructive fire now becomes purifying. A sulphurous thunderbolt destroys Odysseus's companions when they have sinfully eaten the cattle of the sun, and he purifies his house with sulphur after killing the suitors.[32] The fire of the *Odyssey* is that of the hearth and of life itself. On finishing his last battle with the sea and reaching much-spent the land of the Phaeacians, he finds shelter in a fall of olive leaves beneath thick intertwined boughs, as a man on a remote farm shelters a brand beneath the black ash, saving the seed of fire.[33]

Memory of the Mycenaean past descended to a later age not only by the formulae of oral poetry and the recurrent motifs of arming or dining or counseling that guide the narrative, but by more imponderable means. In a logical spirit one may sort stories into legend, myth, and folktale and ascribe to each a characteristic tone. Legend is history—if not quite history as we understand it, yet history nevertheless in its report of people and deeds that later ages, in fear of a kind of orphanhood, would not let die. Myth, though commonly used for the whole body of these stories, in a narrower sense means divine events and, since the gods are in nature, natural events: for example, the sun's white cattle—perhaps the clouds of an otherwise stark sky—which evil people steal or confine and the great Heracles beneficently released. Poseidon's ultimately placated anger against Odysseus states the simple fact that the hero was for ten years lost in the sea. Folktale, harder to define, concerns human and recurrent postures; little Odysseus besting the great Cyclops is first cousin to Jack against the giants and even to Br'er Rabbit against Br'er Fox—our true analogue in a huge world. But though thus divisible in theory, these classes intertwine in fact. Achilles, presumably once actual, in any case fixed in the legendary deed at Troy, takes on the mythical iridescence of his mother the sea-nymph and, in his choice between a long and inglorious and a short glorious life, expresses perfection's transience. The actual Mycenaean world, which in our lifetime emerges more and more clearly into view, was obviously refracted through the prisms of such ways of thinking and narrating, no doubt with progressive distortion as centuries followed the fall of the great centers. Homer's usefulness in reconstituting knowledge of the Mycenaean age depends exactly on how heavily one weighs the conservative as against the refracting force of his oral tradition. We are not here concerned with that lost age, and I ask indulgence for introducing my last summer's impressions, first, of Agamemnon's superb but stark Mycenae, then of Nestor's watered, abundant, sea-commanding, distance-haunted Pylos; their difference seemed almost that between the *Iliad* and the *Odyssey*. In the throne room at Pylos the seated king would once have looked straight down on a tile with a painted octopus, and griffons, half-lion, half-eagle, flanked the throne.[34] The art historian Malraux sees in the claws and teeth of predaceous animals a recurrent art-form of warlike civilizations.[35] The age was certainly that, and the lions of the *Iliad* and of the gate at Mycenae perpetuate the temper. But the fanciful and bright griffons of Pylos, seemingly momentarily resting from the sea and sky, are of another, lighter spirit. When in the *Odyssey* Odysseus at last reaches Ithaca, he stores his possessions in a misty cave near the shore where bees store honey and the naiads weave their sea-purple clothes, a cave with two entrances, one for men, the other for gods. The dimension of space and freedom that speaks in this entrance used by gods appears also in the griffons and the octopus of Pylos; it is the dimension of the *Odyssey* and may have been as true of that vanished age as were the proud Mycenaean lions. But, to return to our present purpose, the means by which this dimension enters the story is that of myth and folktale. In these accounts, ostensibly of geographical travel but actually of travel in experience, the legend of Mycenae opens on horizons stretching beyond history into nature and the mind's movement through it.

Odysseus, the traveler in experience, is obviously as removed in ardor as in age from the young Achilles, and it may be for this reason as much as any that some have denied Homer this second poem, as if the same mind could not admire both men. But people aged even in the youth of the world, and as Shakespeare in the period of his tragedies must have been obsessed by thoughts of the destructiveness and cross-purposes of things, yet lived to the radiant period of the late comedies, so one may imagine Homer as devoured for a time by the flame of heroism that went up in the conflagration of Troy, yet at a later time reaching another mood. It is not after all as if the *Iliad* lacks feeling for the beloved and beautiful securities of life, which shine in Hector's sense of family and city; it is only that no one can keep them. Achilles' final greatness is that he sees his own life, like everything else, sharing the universal loss. Odysseus too accepts his mortality; that is part of his choice in leaving Calypso. Further, it can hardly be accidental that his descent to the underworld comes at the midpoint of his travels. One has the impression that in an earlier tradition the visit was devastating—certainly it is so in *Gilgamesh*[36]—but in our actual *Odyssey* it has something like the tone of privilege, as of lost faces seen again, questions answered, search almost satisfied. The Odysseus who emerges is progressively more alone until, cast up naked at Phaeacia and then mysteriously returned to Ithaca asleep, he comes near to being reborn. Thus he does not ask, as Achilles in youth might almost legitimately have asked, to be immortal; he is content with what he has seen, which is paradoxically of almost godlike width. His mortality is the price of his knowledge.

We began by saying that Homer never doubted the bright reality of his world or thought that only thoughts made it real. Thus when the hurricane throws Odysseus off his homeward course around Cape Malea, the strange world that he enters seems as firm as the familiar world that he has left. Pottery and place names make clear that Mycenaean sailors had in fact sailed west, and they were followed in the late eighth century by Greek colonists. Homer perhaps knew actual accounts of sailors, and down to the present people have not ceased to chart Odysseus's course. Yet, if reported with the color and some substance of a real voyage, it is much more than that, but combines—all in the same sparkling light of fresh discovery—travel in the physical world, among different societies, and in inward, mental regions. He sees the reefs and whirlpool of Scylla and Charybdis, the land of the sun's white cattle, the fjord-like bay of the Laestrygonians—touched surely by some Nordic account—where the paths of day and night are close and a sleepless man might earn two wages, as cattleherd by day and shepherd by night of the flocks of the white sheep.[37] He sees the primitive Cyclopes who live alone without law, city, trade, or agriculture existing on nature's bounty, but also the luxurious Phaeacians, kindred of the gods, suspicious of strangers, and possessed of magic ships that cross the sea without the work of oarsmen or steersmen; they are as far above the social and inventive Greeks as the Cyclopes are below them.[38] He meets the slack-willed Lotuseaters, whose dreamy food brings forgetfulness of home and family, and inhabits Circe's sexual realm. In the Siren's song, the Faustian moment of his travel, he is promised not only knowledge of history in the tale of Troy but knowledge also of how all things come into existence on the much-nourishing earth.[39] Among the dead he gains awareness of a more personal kind from his mother about his family, from Teiresias about his future, from his companions at Troy about their lives then and now; and in contemplating their second state and all the legions of the just and unjust dead, he sees something like the appointed framework of mortal life, yet with Calypso he prefers the identity and life that he can fulfill to nature's anonymous and ageless continuity. All this amounts to something like total travel in the world and in himself, and he changes in the course of it from the shrewd conqueror returning with the loot of Troy to the wise man returning with much richer treasures—treasures that have been freely given, not extorted, the external token and accompaniment of his inner gains. It is said that he secured the chest that the Phaeacians gave him with a knot that he had learned from Circe[40] —which chest and knot express as well as anything else the knowledge that is now his to use.

The bow that in contest with the suitors he alone can string, the token of the bed one leg of which he had long ago made from an olive trunk still rooted in the earth and knowledge of which at the end reveals him securely to Penelope,[41] her weaving and unweaving the web during his uncertain absence, these are tales of arrival as profound as are the others of travel. What in certain moods one can think an impious later tradition made him the perpetual traveler, forever unsatisfied. The point of the *Odyssey* is exactly the opposite. Travel implies home, and the mind's travel the mind's arrival. Even the young Telemachus, in his journeys to Pylos and Sparta with which the poem begins, gains promise that he will grow up to resemble his father; at the end he might with one more attempt, Homer says, have strung his father's bow.[42] The radiant tone of affirmation that surrounds this finally united family differs totally from the fire of consuming heroism that blazed at Troy. We have noted in the Trojan story two stages of spirit: those who lacked courage to attempt the unknown, and those who had courage but lost the day of their home-returning. The *Odyssey* shows a third stage, possible to that tough and lucky mind that can answer the first bright sight of things, survive, and come out the other side, through experience changed to itself and others but with unchanged grip on the brightness that first inspired it.

Chapter Two

THE VISIONARY MIND

We imagined in the first lecture a natural bond between the heroic temper and a gaze that sees the world with sharp and bright particularity. The heart that leaps to the invitation of sparkling appearances is the heart that would itself perform as handsomely. Odysseus at Phaeacia likens Nausicaa to a young palm that he had seen beside Apollo's altar at Delos, and the Trojan Simoesius, killed early in the *Iliad* by Ajax, falls like the white poplar that grew tall in the meadow.[1] This likening of human beings to trees evokes an undivided world in which men and nature share a joint vitality and, initially at least, no shadow falls between them. But needless to say, the shadow will someday fall, and different as they are, Achilles and Odysseus show their greatness in facing much more clearly than others their mortal inability to keep the bright world to which they especially respond. The bleak paradox of heroism, immortal in Achilles, is that the greatest response invites the earliest death. The gods alone keep their ageless sparkle, and the reason why in Homer they can sometimes seem less noble than men is that they need fear no loss. Odysseus, who of all Homeric figures easily comes nearest to seeing life intellectually, will have the serenest death, as if by width of experience he had somehow finally mastered the fierce tug in the brilliant world that draws to brilliant action.

We discussed also the means by which this bright particularity is conveyed—the so-called simple style or what the ancients also called the strung-along style, the *lexis eiromene*. The more complex outlook of the fifth century, which we now approach, reveals itself by more elaborate structures in which ordering thought plays a stronger part and which accordingly fuse the outer show of things more intimately with the mind's conscious response. A general term for these later styles is lacking, since the sweep of Aeschylus and Pindar differs from Sophocles' calm wholeness, but it may be legitimate to call Homer's the style of simile, the later the styles of metaphor. Similes, or Homer's similes at least, keep things apart; metaphors fuse them together. For example, the just-mentioned lines on the death of the Trojan Simoesius read in detail: "Straight through his shoulder the bronze spear went, and he lay in the dust on the ground like a white poplar which sprang smooth in the damp of a wide lowland and its branches grew near the top; a wheelwright with bright iron hewed it down in order to rim the wheel of a beautiful chariot, and it lies withered by the river bank: such was Simoesius the son of Anthemion whom Zeus-descended Ajax cut off." One may contrast the dust of the battlefield where he fell to the watery bank where the tree lies; once the tree is in Homer's mind, the man does not so intrude as to obscure its life and its end, which stand clear in their own right, con-

nected with the man only by their common fall before hard
metal and the end of things formerly tall and alive. A thousand examples would show only more fully Homer's manner
in the similes of keeping things apart, so that for a moment
the action stops and the thing compared emerges for itself
claiming totally its instant of attention. The similes thus make
still more explicit the identities that things have in the epithets; one of the miracles of the style is to evoke a world of
countless existences, each complete, each worth noting. But
contrast to this outlook the famous opening lines of Pindar's
First Olympian Ode: "Excellent is water, and gold like blazing fire shines clear at night above man-ennobling wealth. But
if of games you would sing, dear heart, seek than the sun no
hotter blazing star by day in the empty sky." Without paus-
ing here for Pindar's intention, observe his syntax. The water
stands enigmatically alone, obviously implying some meaning that he gives it; the gold and the fire are so intermixed
as to share the verb "shine clear," and if the fire shines in the
night, the gold likewise does so; then the thought of the
Olympic games prompts mention of his own heart, and the
intolerable sun blazing alone in the stark sky in some way
gives the grounds for his startled self-adjuration. One would
be partly right in calling the difference of all this from anything in Homer the difference between a lyric and a narrative
manner, but there is obviously more. Pindar has personal feelings that burn in his mind; they color his view of objects and
become so fused with them that the water, the gold, the fire,
the games, the sun in the empty sky, though denoting real
things, are also steps and stages of his thought. Such a meta-

phorical style joins together what the Homeric similes hold apart. In reporting of the world, it simultaneously reports opinions about the world. In sum, it comes much closer to reflecting a conscious knowledge that what the mind sees in the world is partly its own meanings.

Now of the many ways of trying to understand a great artistic age, one way is to conceive it as a transient moment when people still see the world primarily through the play and color of action and the senses, not through ideas, yet also as a time when ideas are rising toward the surface, almost but not quite breaking the old reliance on impression. An outlook that speaks chiefly through poetry, drama, and the arts rather than through philosophy and science obviously finds action and impression the main reality. Everything that it reports comes back to what a person observes and feels; otherwise why put on the stage Agamemnon or Oedipus, Hamlet or Lear, declaring in their own words the hard-won response that events wring from them? Socrates of course speaks in Plato, as do statesmen and generals in Thucydides, yet they all express or seek some more or less systematic order that lies outside and beyond themselves and will, if fully understood, clarify the world. In short, they seek reality through ideas; the characters of drama find it in feeling and action. It may again be replied that this is only the difference between drama and the more analytical vehicles of philosophy and history, but the fact remains that the former reflects one kind of age, the latter another kind. Thus a great artistic age is one that lives with the color of the world as people directly feel it; it does not brush aside the show and impression of things in favor of ideas and definitions that are felt to express reality more purely. This is not of course to say that the poetic mind does not think, only that its ideas are not distilled and separated off from emotion and the senses, as if these impeded thought; rather, it works and moves as the consciousness itself seems to do, simultaneously entertaining ideas, sensuous impressions, moral tones, feelings of attraction or dislike, all inextricably bound together and speaking as one. Of all forms of knowledge, literature most closely transcribes the consciousness because it works in this undivided way and does not, like mathematics or a science, buy its gains by isolating that part of the consciousness that deals with recurrences and logical sequences. It approaches things as the eyes and ears— even to some degree, the other senses—together with mind, emotion, and memory approach them, all functioning together. Literature in so doing obviously puts trust in individual experience, as if each person's main function were to respond to life as fully as possible and to learn its teachings by all the means at his command. This brings us back to the character of a great age: it is a time when meanings seem within people's reach. The Athenians who thronged the south slope of the Acropolis to watch a play of Aeschylus, like the Londoners who crowded the pit of the Globe Theatre, clearly did not think that knowledge lay hidden in some esoteric school, to be reached by analysis. Rather, it lay open to the senses and thoughts of daily consciousness; its language was only the fullest use of the common tongue. A great age is a moment of faith and sharing, before the complexities of nature and society separate man from man in a pursuit of special powers that destroys the former faith in the full consciousness.

Such ages are brief because the great events that rouse this mood of hope and vision also beget a bigger society which in turn seems analyzable only through more systematic means. We shall not rehearse here the fall of Peisistratid tyranny in Athens in 510 B.C. (when Aeschylus was fifteen), the invention of democracy under Cleisthenes, the vivid expansion of the next decades, and the crowning affirmations of victory over the Persians at Marathon in 490 and Salamis in 480. Herodotus a half century later praised democracy because when the Athenians served a tyrant they had done nothing remarkable, whereas when free and their own masters they had risen to the first position in Greece.[2] The explanation is no doubt too simple; the spread of trade under the tyrants and the destruction of the old landed order helped bring into being the sense of scope and movement that accompanied the first democracy. The British Tudors have been likened to the Greek tyrants, and the assumption of the monastery lands by Henry VIII and the ensuing growth of trade and opportunity give material grounds to some parallel between the Athenian and the English Renaissance. But the Athenians' very victories over Persia made them champions of Greek freedom. That role put them at the head of the maritime league, the so-called Delian Confederacy, that was brought into being to forestall a third Persian attack, and from it flowed to Athens a power and centrality that with time came to constitute empire with all its complexities.

We shall pursue this era later but return now to the brevity of the great poetic outpouring in Aeschylus, his contemporary the Theban Pindar, and the generation-younger Sophocles. Its mood is a standing mystery, sunlit, humane, marvelous in sweep and range, in touch with the shapes and actions of daily life, yet simultaneously above them in noble ideality. One may show tameness in thinking all very beautiful things mysterious, as if from expectation of colorlessness and surprise at the exception. The mystery lies not only in the created works but even more in the outlook that prompted them. As we have seen, the mind of such an age surely thought, not through analyzed ideas, but through ideas interfused with the full play of the senses. For the Greeks a chief impulse to such a way of thinking was the great skein of legend, myth, and folktale discussed earlier; people had known it from childhood and it was lodged in their lives, conveying at once the past, the outflung shapes and happenings of nature, the acts of gods, and the numberless attitudes and stances with which people met the world. One must imagine that, in confronting present events, not just the poets but—insofar as they spoke for the general mind—everyone had recourse to this great panorama of reality, more or less unconsciously referring to it what they personally underwent. The mythology was a kind of language, and since Greek religion hinged not on doctrine but on act and cult, even the received tales about the gods could change as fresh insight prompted. But, chiefly, it was mythology that supplied a way of seeing reality in the full color of the senses. The legendary stories showed men acting in a visible world and under pressing circumstances, yet were beyond the present in a realm where actions might

be isolated and moral shapes stand clear. The mythology was
wide enough—seemingly as wide as life itself—to include
nearly all conceivable postures; it was, in short, a form of
human knowledge. But everything depended on people's will
to see the present under this inclusive light. When outlooks
changed and men wanted to analyze the present for itself, or
to penetrate nature, or to define grounds of conduct more exactly, the bright skein faded and minds no longer wove with
it. Another kind of world came into existence, a world of
concepts rather than figures, of prose rather than verse, of
analysis rather than myths. It is accordingly possible to divide
Greek thought into two periods, the mythological and the
conceptual. Part of the grip on the imagination that fifth-
century Athens never ceases to hold is that these two kinds
of worlds met then, the former culminating as the latter came
into being. Aeschylus and Sophocles spoke for the older outlook that saw things through shape; Socrates and Thucydides
for the nascent mind that saw them through idea.

The practice early existed in Athens by which each of three
competitors at the spring festival of the Great Dionysia sub-
mitted three tragedies and a satyr play, a so-called tetralogy.
Unlike his successors, Aeschylus seems habitually to have
treated one mounting theme in each such sequence, notably
in the first three plays, the so-called trilogy. His *Persians* is
the one extant exception. This fact in itself tells something
about him: he was interested in time and process. Further,
to judge by our extant trilogy, the *Oresteia,* and by fragments
of the plays that continued the trilogies of the *Prometheus
Bound* and the *Suppliants,* the process that thus engaged him

was progressive; it verged to solutions, and time was the great teacher. Since we have only seven of his some ninety attested plays, we are hardly in a position to say that he always held this bright faith in history's instruction; yet that he wrote in sequences makes certain that he thought in greater movements than any character could grasp or express in a given play. Since only the gods survey continuity, he is the most visionary of the dramatists in tracking the unfolding purposes of Zeus and showing the longer light that surrounds the opaque present.

This bent of mind must reflect his own experience and, so far as we may judge from him, the temper of the new democracy. It is ironic that the Athenians, who invented democracy, left so ambiguous a record of it. Because political theory did not take full form until the troubled years of the Peloponnesian War, Aeschylus almost alone gives voice to the bold first mood when democracy transformed Athens. Though by education we remain pupils of the conceptual age of Greece and more easily recognize political ideas in the analyzing prose of Thucydides and Plato than in the verse and myths of Aeschylus, yet political ideas inform these, and the confident progress that speaks in the trilogies is the progress that shone in Athens. It shows not only in the fact of his sequences but in the vision of time and space that they reveal. Thirty thousand years, a commentator says,[3] elapsed for the Prometheus of our play before he rose from beneath the earth toward his reconciliation with Zeus—so long had the harsh primal hate persisted—and the *Oresteia* traces the progress from Agamemnon's self-assertive will to wealth and conquest, through Clytemnestra's guilty obsession with house and family, to Orestes' final freedom in the reconciling judgment of the court of the Areopagus in Athens. Space to Aeschylus is time's concomitant. Xerxes' vast army in the *Persians* draws from all quarters of the populous east; the fugitive daughters of Danaus in the *Suppliants* import to Argos tones of misty Egypt; Prometheus from his rock sees the nations of men; Clytemnestra in the *Agamemnon* spies the progress of the beacon fires that announce at home the sack of distant Troy; in search of purgation Orestes travels the Greek world. If the impenetrable mind of Zeus works through time and space, Aeschylus in trying to reach that mind is drawn to like dimensions. Some of his figures, notably Prometheus, suggest Michelangelo's, except that Aeschylus does not so much express sheer human power as the scope that such power naturally seeks. Yet his scope characteristically merges at the end with community; it is the Athenian Areopagus that in Orestes puts to rest at last the long guilt of the family of Pelops. In this final coming home to institutions and, if not to the present, at least to a continuing bond with it is to be heard the voice of the actual democracy. If space is conceived as the mind's free dimension and place as the actual setting where, since we are not gods, our limited lives must be worked out, then freedom seems for Aeschylus some sort of merging of space with place. Place prescribes natural bounds which space draws outward toward growth and inclusiveness. The events of his lifetime showed the possibility of this bright interworking, and the trilogies trace its slow emergence.

Let us pursue the process, though briefly, in the *Oresteia*.

The trilogy consists of three plays, *Agamemnon, Choephoroe,* and *Eumenides*; it covers two generations and suggests a third. Though at the start the watchman on the roof of the palace at Mycenae awaits and soon sees the beacon that declares the fall of Troy, the chorus of old men promptly carries attention from the end to the beginning of the great expedition. Agamemnon and his brother Menelaus, they say, resembled eagles shrieking in the sky for justice at the rifling of their nest—Paris's theft of Helen—and a god heard the birds' cry.[4] Yet at the actual departure, they go on, two eagles were in fact seen devouring a pregnant hare, which portent the seer Calchas interpreted to mean both gain and loss: gain in the promise of victory, loss in the anger of the virgin goddess Artemis at the destruction of things weak and innocent.[5] This intermixture of success with blood and guilt marks the early stages of the trilogy, and Agamemnon's royal greatness signifies of former monarchy a violence that accompanied its glory. Contrast this view of Agamemnon to the sight of him in the final book of the *Odyssey*: Homer saw in him the exemplar of an imperfect though seemingly glorious human fate, Aeschylus sees in him the guilt of an imperfect historical era. The one surveys paradigms of lives, the other paradigms of history. It is a disputed question whether the angry Artemis, by creating the calm at Aulis and forcing Agamemnon in placation to sacrifice his daughter Iphigenia, in effect robs him of all choice, or whether, conversely, the portent describes rather than compels the king's mind. Under the latter interpretation, his warlike mood shows in his preference of army over daughter and conquest over innocence. He in any case took the dire step, and the chorus, aware that guilt has consequences, yet eager for peace and the army's return, is left to brood on the unsearchable will of Zeus—"He who guides mankind to sobriety, who made sovereign learning by suffering. There steeps from sleep before the heart pain's memory of pain; even the reluctant reach sobriety. The kindness of the gods is done through force from their calm steering-seat."[6] The doctrine of learning through suffering, thus announced, imperfectly fits some of the characters—notably Agamemnon in his quick death on his return—but it applies to the audience, too, who see in the trilogy the cost of violence and the long path to its transcendence. War in the *Agamemnon* lacks Homeric glory. A messenger who precedes the king's return describes the innumerable deaths and the tedium of summers and winters through the long years at Troy,[7] and the chorus connects the theft of Helen and the impulse to retrieve her through war with the heart's insouciant will to get what it wants—a child chasing a flying bird[8]—and further connects this insouciance with wealth. Justice, they say, shines in smoke-stained houses but flees halls decked with gold.[9] When the returning king is greeted flatteringly by his leonine wife Clytemnestra and is invited to step from his chariot upon a purple carpet,[10] the royal dye comes to signify the wealth and glory which contained his guilt; and when she murders him after his bath helpless in lengths of swathing cloth, its coils comprise such another net of retribution as he had cast over Troy. History is inexorable, and the gods enforce its instruction through pain.

The Trojan Cassandra who returned with him as prize and

concubine makes clear a sexual side in this pursuit of glory. She is to him much what Helen is to Menelaus and Paris, the flying bird that the child can never catch. Clytemnestra, too, though she claims to avenge on Agamemnon the sacrifice of their daughter Iphigenia, has her own paramour in Aegisthus, the king's home-staying cousin. One of the chief terms of the trilogy is this war of the sexes. Agamemnon, in preferring the army and the expedition to his daughter's life, asserted a masculine will to power which destroys the fertile continuity of nature, much as the eagles destroyed the pregnant hare. Before her death Cassandra with second sight sees the adultery, the child killing, and the cannibalism that in the generation before had marked the struggle for power between the fathers of Agamemnon and Aegisthus. Though they claim to be righting these past wrongs, Clytemnestra and Aegisthus in fact waded to power through further crime, and when Cassandra enters the fatal house to her own death, the chorus cries: "Mortal prosperity is insatiable. At palaces that every finger points to never a voice gives check crying 'Do not go in.' "[11] The palace in effect becomes royalty itself, and royalty the male appetitiveness that does not shrink at violating nature for its wishes. Aeschylus, though he fought at Marathon and passed to later generations as the spokesman of unspoiled fighting valor, disliked and distrusted the celebrated age of the heroes as self-seeking, heedless of civic ties, destructive of the female element of continuity and increase.

The bonds of society and family thus outraged in the *Agamemnon* are done as great violence in the *Choephoroe* but in a different way. Thucydides later said that self-concern robbed the Greek tyrants of adventurousness,[12] and something of this inlooking, house-regarding tone surrounds the second play. For all her intransigence, Clytemnestra is feminine in her fixity on the house; Aegisthus is twice called a tyrant;[13] and if the first play described the old monarchic age, this play describes the age of tyranny that followed. Even Clytemnestra's death has an interior quality that contrasts to Agamemnon's worldly scope. She dreamed that when she put her child to her breast, it became a snake that bit her.[14] Orestes, brought up at Delphi far from home, accepts on his return the snake's secrecy. He says that Apollo had warned him of leprous impairment and withering if he should fail of his duty;[15] he has no way backward, only forward. He in fact falters when, admitted to the house on a false story of his own death, he first kills Aegisthus, then confronts his mother; but he is steeled by his friend Pylades with a reminder of Apollo's command[16] and does the hateful act. He had at least grown up removed from wealth and power, and at this dark center of the trilogy the action seems to move still farther inward to a region of the naked will alone. Agamemnon's violent crimes at home and abroad have shrunk in Clytemnestra and Aegisthus to the narrow regimen of the household, and if the male will alone was destructive, so is the female.

The solution will evidently lie in some form of harmony, and its slow emergence in the *Eumenides* has the colors of dawn. The memory of pain that in the chorus of the *Agamemnon* seeps into the heart at night and in the *Choephoroe* roused Clytemnestra with nightmare will end with the daylight of reason. The Furies, now the chorus, pursue Orestes in the name of the taboo against murder within the family, on which grounds Clytemnestra's murder of her husband was of no concern to them since the two were not related by blood.[17] In opposition to them Apollo, Orestes' original champion, defends him on the ground that voluntary compacts outweigh inheritance,[18] hence that by higher and more civilized standards Clytemnestra's crime is the worse. This confrontation between old and new gods still contains the conflict between female and male, the one in continuity, the other in will and choice. The many-sided resolution is partly in Orestes himself, who goes through some four stages: first clinging to Apollo's altar with his guilt freshly on him and his bloody sword still in hand, then finding in travel and men's acceptance some remove from the horror, then hearing in Apollo's advocacy before the Areopagus the rational ground of his action, finally in Athena's favorable decision reaching, as it were, the actuality of freedom, a kind of rebirth.[19] From a public and social point of view, she—the goddess of Athens —is by far the main force. Though as her father's solely created child she tips the even vote of the Areopagus in favor of the male principle[20]—which is to say, the principle of rational and accountable choice—she is able to do so without, like Apollo, alienating the ancient Furies, who express not the chosen but the given and inborn force of inheritance. Her influence on them achieves in effect a mixture of reason with inheritance—or, in our previous terminology, of space with place—and they change at the end to become the Benignant Ones, Eumenides, principles of fertility and continuity. They share with her the last word: let no blight, they sing, infect bud and blossom, let girls find husbands, children grow up strong, honor and accord reign, hymns rise at smoking altars.[21] Their paean to blooming nature expresses an accord that is both historical and personal. Historically, the rule of law personified in the Areopagus will have replaced the personal rule of monarchs and tyrants with the promise of a juster and more rational state. Individually, the old wealth that signified self-aggrandizement will yield to the innocent wealth of field, family, and city. Female continuity and male force will be reconciled in some sort of union between commitment and choice, retention and creation, past and future. In this personal sense, the burden of the trilogy is more than historical; it describes a possible creativity that works with rather than against nature and by sympathy rather than by self-assertion.

A summary of a great and complex work, even in the unlikely event of its not distorting the true emphasis, wholly lacks the breath of the original. But the problem of understanding such a work is not at bottom that it was written to be heard at a remote time and in a foreign tongue, but, as we have kept saying, that it speaks for a mind that saw reality through shape rather than through idea. In this respect the Greek dramatists differ even from the Elizabethan, since in the written legacy of medieval learning the latter had ways of regarding the state, the church, history, law, monarchy, and much else, whereas for the Greeks such analytical conquests were yet to come and the dramatists surveyed a less charted terrain. Though all literature is synoptic and the sentient mind makes what it can of its total present, one is justified in saying that the Greek poets had a particularly central and public task because they virtually alone expressed the main structures of society. Thus it is not enough to say that the *Oresteia* concerns intense characters at moments of revelation; these characters have the further function of elucidating society and showing its nature in their own. This function gives to early Greek poetry its characteristically public tone. Shakespeare, too, has that tone, but it is set in a subtlety of language that declares the center of his art to lie in the inward consciousness, not in the public function. Aeschylus's emphasis is much more evenly poised between the personal and the social. A summary of the *Oresteia* thus has at least the merit of emphasizing through brevity the wider resonance of the characters toward something like history itself, and more than toward history, toward the living state that Athenians were in the process of making. Aeschylus is the spokesman of time's instruction. Its teaching is that suffering gives knowledge,[22] and suffering is not to him only the iron law by which Agamemnon and Clytemnestra died for their crimes, but the method of Zeus himself to lead Athenians, both individually and as a state, to a juster creativity.

But if this or something like this is the trilogy's teaching, then the metaphorical bent of mind that sees objects in a joint light and spies overlapping meanings in the world shows itself not only in Aeschylus's language but in his very purpose. That is surely the case. Homer's way of seeing the world as flashing with bright particulars has yielded now to a complexer, more mental vision to which the world forever presents similarities and hints at underlying laws. The eagles of the start of the *Agamemnon* wheeling in the sky and crying for vengeance become in the two later eagles of the portent analogues of the warlike kings; the prophet Calchas marks the link, but prophecy is now a form of metaphor, and the predacity of the eagles then extends to the ruin of Troy, the death of Iphigenia, and the Mycenaean kingship itself; Orestes and Electra in the *Choephoroe* call themselves eaglets that would regain their nests.[23] The trilogy is knit together by such recurring figures of speech. The blow by which Agamemnon struck down Troy recurs in his death;[24] so does the net, which extends even to the Furies' tracking of Orestes;[25] the light that the watchman on the roof first awaits shines deceptively to each main character in his moment of apparent success,[26] to shine permanently at last only in the torches that guide the Eumenides to their benign cult. The night in which remembered pain rouses the sleeper becomes something like error's long night, and sexual violence and adventure describe its uneasiness. All this and much more shows a mind that seeks order and meaning, not conceptually, but rather through a thousand sibylline appearances that seem to share some common secret and half conceal, half reveal the laws of things. If Homer keeps the youth of the world, Aeschylus keeps the youth of intellect, marvelous in its freshness of search and its faith that search is rewarded.

Only Pindar among the poets and Heraclitus as a forerunner of the philosophers shared the full sweep of this confidence. They mark, as it were, extremes of which Aeschylus is the mean: Heraclitus in imperious scorn of the world of appearances and desire to rouse men from the sleep of the senses

to the mind's waking;[27] Pindar in a quite opposite devotion
to the flush and show of games and cults and festivals, yet
with an attendant sense that divinity shines in these and that
great moments of life give intimations of the gods. The verses
considered earlier on water, gold like fire at night, and the
sun blazing in the empty sky cryptically formulate this faith.[28]
Water in other odes evokes to him the poetry of festal moments after the strain of effort,[29] when vision is clear and the
inspiration and sanction of effort in gods and heroes rise before the mind. Night elsewhere is obscurity, from which heroic courage blazes with the gold of divine favor,[30] and if the
sun in the empty sky fits for him the matchless brightness of
Olympic victory, it has in the thought of Zeus something for-
bidding also, since mortals cannot endure its full blaze. He
speaks elsewhere of the bronze sky that men cannot climb,
and Zeus's unattainability is in this passage and ode.[31] Yet the
golden example of heroes remains, and something of their
god-given timelessness shines, he thinks, in all moments of
great success, as a like completeness shines for Heraclitus in
the harmony that resolves opposites and the wheel of the elements that maintains the world.[32] Like Aeschylus, both see
in passing things an intimation of things permanent, and
through much the same means, which is the bold trust that
the senses hint at realities behind them. If plays are more
pressing than victory odes or cryptic philosophic statements,
it is because Athenian politics were more pressing. The process of change that had produced democracy drew from the
past, and though it had begotten a better world than Agamemnon knew, it had still to cope with the passions. It is to

these that Aeschylus's doctrine of learning through suffering is directed. The purgation of the passions that Aristotle found in tragedy has a social aim in Aeschylus, and his new Athens is to consist of tempered citizens.

Finally, Sophocles both completes and contracts this spacious vision. Form is limit, and the most achieved form implies some contraction. Among the four plays that according to Attic practice he would produce at a given Dionysia, there is no record that any were in sequence. Rather, each was complete in itself, and the fact has an opposite implication from Aeschylus's trilogies: namely, that he saw life, not as process and change, but as situation. He was not, like Aeschylus, the child of the Athenian revolution but saw the democracy as achieved and its triumphs as evident; hence he was less interested in promise than in actuality. The irreducible, granitic base was for him the situations at which strong natures arrive through their very strength—moments from which there is no escape through change or time but which in themselves contain and reveal all that there is. Hence his single plays each show a single destiny. When one tries to imagine Sophocles' youth and the impression on him that Aeschylus's sweeping trilogies must have made, there seems something inspired in the self-fidelity which told him that such wide prospects were not for him; his reality would be narrower, more urgent, more interior. He did not apparently see the full implications at once; what are thought to be his earlier plays—the *Ajax, Antigone,* and *Trachiniae*—break near the middle with the death of the protagonist, almost as if they were small trilogies showing both an action and its consequences. The *Oedipus*

Tyrannus from a formal point of view is justly thought his masterpiece because attention beats cumulatively on a single character; the play belongs totally to the protagonist, and form and substance are perfectly at one. But the formal difference is only of degree, and from first to last each play shows the iron moment to which a life has led and from which there is no turning. In Sophocles the humanism that marks all Greek art and thought is most complete. Gods surround his dramatic actions in the sense that time and destiny frame all events, and each character unsparingly illumines a way of life and cast of thought, but the fact does not from the character's point of view blunt exigency or soften decision. "A man's character is his destiny," said Heraclitus,[33] and the plays illustrate the judgment. The humanistic Aristotle therefore found the perfection of tragedy in Sophocles;[34] Aeschylus's more inchoate and theological vision must have seemed to him relatively unformed. Sophocles indeed completes Aeschylus, not in the sense of carrying farther, but rather in accepting a present that Aeschylus had seen in process of creation and stating plainly what it holds.

His long life of ninety-one years spanned the fifth century. An Athenian general in middle life, friend of Pericles, Herodotus, and doubtless nearly all the great figures of the age, he was thought fortunate to die a year before the defeat of Athens by Sparta, the capture of the city, and the end of that greatest period of her long life. Hence he surely felt the intellectual revolution that accompanied his middle and late years—what we have called the substitution of conceptual for mythological thought. Protagoras and Anaxagoras were roughly the same age as he, Democritus a few years younger, and Socrates a quarter-century younger. The structure of the plays shows intellectual refinement; the *Antigone,* for example, is cut like a diamond into facets of antithesis: between the strong and the weaker sister, Antigone and Ismene; between father and son, Creon and Haemon; and centrally between Creon and Antigone, the one vindicating the state, the other the family. And yet this intellectual influence, however strong, seems at bottom not to have touched, much less to have impaired, his mythological cast of mind; it simply chiseled and refined it, as if by opposition it made it more aware of itself. The result was a kind of distillation of mythological moments and characters to their essence. The legendary heroes had given the Greeks from Homer on a gallery of representative lives which stood simultaneously within and beyond history: within it because they were believed to have lived, beyond it because they had risen through poetry to the plane of the illustrative. This legacy both of actual legend and, more important, of a mythological way of seeing things became in Sophocles what we mean by the classic: figures half within, half beyond time, identifiable as unique men and women yet more than that, not at all allegories of ideas because they fully live, yet representative of permanent human stances toward self and society—in sum, figures from whom the accidental and the minor have been so pared away that the organic structure of a life stands whole. This is the full flower of the outlook that we have pursued so far, complete in the poise of the conceived figure and in the depth of the imagined situation. Homer's sparkling scope and Aeschylus's visionary progress are gone, replaced by classic representativeness.

Pericles, the first figure in Athens as a statesman and even in part as a thinker, died in 429, in the third year of the Peloponnesian War, from the plague that attended the crowding of the city by fugitives fleeing the invading Spartans. He had advocated accepting the risk of war on the ground that invasion would not in the long run protect Sparta against the Athenian naval power; the plague had been his only miscalculation. Partly because plague sets the situation of the *Oedipus Tyrannus,* partly on one or two technical grounds of structure,[35] partly because the intellectual Oedipus also made confident predictions, the play should probably be dated in these dark years. But one must not at all equate Oedipus with Pericles, or see in the king a portrait of the statesman. Surely that was not how Sophocles' mind worked. If the essence of events had been the failure of even the best intelligence to penetrate the future and it was clear that the gods do what they will with mortal plans, this fact had its archetype in Oedipus. Sophocles was indeed concerned with the present but on another plane, a plane where Oedipus lived his own life and followed his own nature. Yet to think of Sophocles as writing for art alone is to think of him in a vacuum apart from the intense life of Athens. He both shared that life and transcended it in the timelessness of legend, where acts followed from their own necessity and shapes took on what Aristotle later called a philosophic reality.[36]

It is impossible to convey the tension of the *Oedipus Tyrannus* and doubtless foolish to try. The play concerns in essence the conflict between the pragmatic and the visionary life, and its terminology turns on sight. Thus the seeing king first opposes the blind prophet Teiresias, and all the seemingly secure but ultimately uncertain confidence of the man of action facing the unknown future speaks in the scene. Teiresias ends by asking Oedipus whether he knows who his father and mother are,[37] but the question at first simply cracks the king's confidence. The crack widens as his every effort to find the murderer of the former king and the cause of the present pollution leads seemingly by chance back to himself. He is loved and admired for having formerly solved the riddle of the destructive sphinx; no one except the seer Teiresias, least of all his wife Jocasta, thinks of accusing him; it is only that questions almost of their own accord verge toward him. All Sophoclean heroes reach their fate not through weakness but through strength, and he is no exception. When he at last approaches the answer and in a heartrending scene misunderstands Jocasta, who is now aware of the truth and tries to dissuade him from pressing farther,[38] he persists through sheer integrity of mind. As everyone knows—and knew when Sophocles wrote—Oedipus himself proves to be the man who in ignorance killed his father and married his mother. The very force that made him the great man that he was derived obscurely from the insistence of his insecure search. When he tears out his eyes at the end, he in effect becomes one with Teiresias in seeing reality with something like divine sight as reality is, not with mortal sight as he had thought and wished it to be. It was his force, hence his insecurity, that took him from one stage of understanding to the next, and the riddle of his own life proved more dangerous than the riddle of the sphinx. Yet the answer told him who he was, and the discovery, though outwardly ruinous, was the greater triumph.

Aristotle thought every organism naturally attracted toward its fulfillment, and in Sophocles the mythological way of thought with which we have been concerned confirms the law. From Homer on, this way of thought had elicited clear shapes from the changing tangle of events, reducing multiplicity to main lines of order, tracing simplifications in nature and history. The Greek mind first of all sought clarity. In turning from the wide reaches of Homer and Aeschylus, Sophocles substituted depth for scope, representativeness for movement, lapidary form for long horizons. The change was less of direction than of degree, as Homer's Achilles and Odysseus, Aeschylus's Prometheus and Agamemnon and Clytemnestra, make clear—they too stand above events, as it were expressing in their persons the illustrative meaning of their lives. But Sophocles more steadily seeks this classic representativeness, and his Ajax and Antigone, Oedipus and Electra, become each almost a statue of a fate and of a stance toward it. The language of myth has its peculiar eternity, an eternity of which Sophocles was evidently made more conscious by the pressure of change in the Athens of his time. It is a paradox that in Sophocles Greek mythic thought reached its crest just as it was about to fall and shatter—somewhat as his Oedipus at the end meets a reality that will negate what he has been.

Chapter Three

THE THEORETICAL MIND

We have so far followed, first in Homer, then in Aeschylus and Sophocles, two stages of the Greek mind, proceeding on the assumption that the eye and the mind collaborate toward joint meanings and that people make of the world what they see in it. We further assumed that language steadily intervenes as a kind of travel agent, telling the mind where the eye has found routes and stopping places. The mind cannot, so to speak, visit any places that language does not put on the itinerary; we see in the world—or at least consciously see—only what words allow us to. For if we had no word for something, how could we know that we had seen it? The still further assumption has existed that our own and present eyes, and hence our minds, keep sympathies derived from our past stages of life. The pristine freshness that in Homer clothes the world and the innumerable people and objects in it once shimmered for each of us. However far we have traveled from that first shining sight, it can still wake recognition. Hence Homer keeps reality, not at bottom because his blind gaze still saw the Mycenaean past which the Greeks had lost for five centuries, but because everything that he describes keeps a flashing concreteness and beautiful knowability such as we once felt. But whereas we through education were led on to more complex and intellective realities, he traced to its proper conclusion the clarity with which he started. To his vision, the fact of death intruding upon the brilliant world begat heroism in Achilles, a long search toward peace and home in Odysseus. Homer tells us of our world as it would be if we still saw it without books and theories, as we did in youth and in moments still do. Such a belief, to be sure, may be flattering to us, since it involves still another assumption: namely, that if our world were as definite as his, it would still be as wide. Definiteness often sinks into rigidity. This is one way of approaching Homer's mystery: to conceive him as not blurring through theory the sharp outlines of things, yet seeing them with inexhaustible curiosity and feeling. The oral tradition, by providing him with words and even with themes, doubtless helped keep his sight sharp; yet his combined freshness and depth of gaze remained his own, and remain ours too insofar as he recalls us to a kind of primal confrontation with the outspread visible world.

With Aeschylus and Sophocles we entered another world, in which mind and eyes were more nearly partners. Because characters on a stage are visible and myths remained for the dramatists the realm where fates and characters stand clearest, these men evidently continued to think through the medium of the senses, not at all eliminating the color and play of the world as hostile to thought—on the contrary, accepting these as thought's native hue. Yet, unlike Homer, they inter-

fused with impression the guiding lines of intellect. The conflict between Antigone and Creon almost crosses into analysis
of the state, and Oedipus all but phrases the nexus between
insecurity and mental search. Needless to say, the dramatists
did not take the final step that would have carried them from
myth into pure idea; Antigone and Oedipus remain people—
admittedly a special kind of people, more illustrative, closer
to essentials, set in more revealing circumstances than those
of common life, yet people nevertheless. If drama and fiction
always present things in the mixed light of vision and idea,
the position of these early Greek writers was nevertheles sin-
gular; lacking an express, elaborated body of theory to work
against, they had to rise from impression to idea by sheer un-
aided flight. As already noted, Shakespeare was far more conscious of theories about monarchy, the state, the soul, and
much else than Aeschylus could have been, and if Dante's
command of the theology of his age may present an extreme
case, it puts the contrast to the Greeks most clearly. The Greek
dramatists, looking at the world with a complex interworking of mind and eye, elaborated by this means alone their
mighty structures. Their greater complexity, relative to Homer, partly betrays mere time and change. Though even to
Homer Mycenae was long past, the archetypal world of the
heroes was still farther removed from the Athenian writers,
and their present was drastically new. The bygone heroes, if
they were to remain relevant at all, had necessarily to speak
in more synoptic tones, expressing by sheer centrality of stance
and character their bearing on the changed present. Concomi-
tantly, ordinary and visible things such as we saw in the

Oresteia—light, the sexes, eagles, the net, the blow, the palace—could take on through metaphor the double function of expressing real and ideal meanings. Idea was allying itself more and more intimately with impression, and eyes did not merely see but gave language to thought. Aeschylus and Sophocles could not have known in quite our language what they were saying; for if they had known, they would already have thought in the conceptual mode of Socrates and Plato, and their language of myth would have perished. As it is, their mythical characters and situations keep their own imperishable language, asserting through shape what idea is never able to catch quite so suggestively.

We turn now to a kind of twilight when ideas, clearly formulated as such, had indeed come into existence, yet something like the old flash and presentness of the senses remained. In the last lecture, we shall go on to the full victory of concept in Plato and Aristotle. They went far toward creating our present world, and our education still traces in broad outline the panorama of analyzed reality that they formulated. But let us now consider two intermediary figures, Euripides and Thucydides, whom we may regard the more feelingly because, like many of us, they stood between two worlds, dazzled by ideas yet never quite willing to cut the bonds of sense. Euripides, probably born in the middle 480's and before Salamis, was the elder by twenty-five or more years; he was in fact only a decade younger than Sophocles, but like many future iconoclasts he seems later than he was. Whether by age or temperament or for unknown reasons, he seems just to have missed Sophocles' ability to see things wholly by myth; he was attracted to the reasoning of the then rising sophists and was intoxicated by the possibility of reducing human situations to ideas, yet could not escape the grip of myth and wrote plays that are a curious hybrid of situation and concept. Conversely, Thucydides, a young man in his twenties, possibly his early twenties, at the outbreak in 431 of the great war between Athens and Sparta,[1] seems to have thought that he would be able to reduce its future course to a kind of theorem and write a paradigm of wars between great states. Yet at the same time he strongly felt the claims of actuality, and he ended with an account of the war that unites idea with personal, almost visual involvement. Different as they are, these men similarly express the competing claims of complexity and simplification in describing their worlds.

Let us first pause briefly with the Athens of the middle and late fifth century. Politically, her leadership of the Delian Confederacy, the defensive league of Aegean cities that was created soon after Salamis, verged—or so her enemies alleged —toward tyranny as the fear of Persia receded. By the charter of the league a city might contribute either money or ships and men, and Thucydides judged it the glaring fault of many cities that they chose the slacker course of payment rather than of service.[2] The funds thus contributed poured into Athens, providing a continuing stimulus to shipbuilding, trade, and many other kinds of employment, notably on the war fleet. The city, which had been occupied and partly burned by Xerxes in 480 before Salamis and again by his general Mardonius in 479 before Plataea, responded the more sharply

to the challenge as a result of her break with the past. From
an economic point of view it is hard to see how, having once
produced a naval power sufficient to keep Persia from the
Aegean, Athens could have returned, when the danger receded, to her earlier half-agrarian status. In an ideal world
the Delian Confederacy might have become a working government like the Achaean League of two centuries later; as
it was, Athens was its controlling center and the Athenian
assembly in effect its despot. This mounting change was the
more drastic because the city itself was being progressively
transformed from a pleasant market town into a metropolis—
the first that the Greeks had known, and marked by both the
brilliance and the tensions native to big cities. This transformation was in turn the necessary setting of that intellectual
change with which we have been concerned: the change from
verse to prose, from shape to concept, from story to analysis,
from mythological to conceptual ways of thinking. The sophists who flocked to Athens from the 440's on played a double
role, at once toward inquiry and toward rhetoric. The Socrates of Aristophanes' *Clouds* lampoons less the man than the
breed; he hangs in a basket near the ceiling in order to ex-
amine the heavenly bodies at closer range, but also teaches an
ambitious youth how to cheat a jury and outargue his father.
The philosopher Anaxagoras, the friend of Pericles, is said by
Plutarch to have shown by autopsy that a one-horned ram
which was thought a portent simply had a deformed skull.[3]
The earliest writings of the Hippocratic corpus proclaim a
sharp advance, if not so much in the treatment of disease, at
least in observation and prognosis;[4] the astronomer Meton

substituted a solar for the old lunar calendar; the city-planner
Hippodamus laid out streets in the growing Piraeus; the
sculptor Polyclitus defined in his so-called canon an ideal
theoretical relationship between parts of the body.[5] Athenian
life no longer seemed comprehensible through inherited pre-
cept and tried example but called for analytical powers that
looked beneath the visible surface. Thucydides' generation,
which grew up near the outbreak of the Peloponnesian War,
particularly felt the change, and the young men of Plato's
dialogues canvassing abstractions with Socrates repeat in a
more favorable light the youth of Aristophanes' *Clouds* who
learns to confute his father. The illumination that they sought
drew from theory, not from myth and adage. The thrusting
metropolis, unlike the small city of the first democracy in
which Sophocles grew up, still less like the town surround-
ing the Peisistratid court which Aeschylus knew as a boy, was
swept forward by new forces—political, social, intellectual—
against which it had, so to speak, no immunity. The marvel
is not that Athens declined from her great years, but that the
greatness lasted so long.

This or something like this was the city that Euripides was
born into, mirrored, and helped create. If he was born in the
middle 480's, he was forty when the Parthenon was begun in
447. Protagoras, the great precursor of the sophists, was already well known in Athens; so was Herodotus, and possibly
Democritus. The tension between old and new, between myth
and concept, can then seem evenly poised. Phidias's gold and
ivory Athena and the famous marbles of the Parthenon share
the Sophoclean ideality of lifting the shapes of common life

to a changeless plane, where they stand outside of time—classic, essential, almost Olympian. But the empirically minded Protagoras is quoted as saying, presumably in these years, "We cannot know of the gods whether they exist or do not exist, or of what sort they are. Much prevents: the obscurity of the subject and the brevity of human life."[6] Phidias's figures breathe confident possession, Protagoras's sentence expresses uncertain search, and these opposing attitudes are curiously mingled in Socrates, born in 470 and some fifteen years younger than Euripides. He called himself a midwife: declaring himself ignorant, he continually but (as he thought) vainly sought to bring absolutes to clear and present birth. Yet he never doubted the possibility of this birth, and he was secure, if not in attaining final truths, at least in pursuing them. In cast of mind, Euripides stands much nearer the skeptical Protagoras, yet as a playwright he tacitly expressed faith in the old art of seeing things tangibly represented and almost present. He is the opposite of Socrates, doubtful of finalities, drawn to the visible present, distrustful of myths yet in the last analysis wedded to them.

His *Hippolytus,* produced in 428, perhaps within a year of the *Oedipus Tyrannus,* on the surface has much in common with it. Both plays at least stand at far remove from the trilogies of Aeschylus in treating at close range a single circumstance that illuminates the main characters and brings to view in a moment of recognition all that they have lived by. Hence both plays are humanistic in implication, not because they lack awareness of gods but because they find the final measure of things in a man's life; the Aeschylean trilogies say the opposite, that the final measure is the gods' guiding laws. Yet with this much in common, the *Hippolytus* and the *Oedipus Tyrannus* differ profoundly. Though the difference is not easy to define, it seems to have chiefly to do with the relative weight in the world that a man's life may be thought to have. In spite of the terrible revelation of the *Oedipus Tyrannus,* the king ends at a new stage of knowledge, which is fitly marked by his self-blinding as a sign of change from outward to inward sight; moreover, he remains in control, if not of his fate, at least of his response, and the fact leaves him still erect against circumstance, as if attesting that his humanity consisted exactly in his power to keep learning. In his example, a man stands with dignity, even with nobility, in the changing world of natural events, not a god but the gods' fit concern, and tragedy, though destructive of health, strength, wealth, and position, does not destroy but reveals and enhances what is most truly himself. It is in this sense that Sophocles shares the ideality of Phidias's marble figures; his Oedipus and Antigone and Ajax stand above change, humane, portrayed for their essentials, adorning the world, not in essence adorned by it.

But with Euripides a subtle change takes place. When the young hero of the *Hippolytus* first enters, he sees the images of two goddesses, Artemis and Aphrodite: the one virginal and cool, a deity of the woods and hills, removed from mortal heat; the other the goddess of passion, inspirer of birth and change, enemy of isolation, underminer of self-sufficiency. To some unknown extent the two figures seem quite simply to have expressed for Euripides, much as for ourselves, identi-

fiable natural and emotional forces; he was not religious in
any ordinary sense, and the unfolding action conveys in Hippolytus and his stepmother Phaedra an almost automatic response to the respective goddesses. Phaedra's passion for her
stepson and his young, impervious absorption in hunting on
the hills and riding on vacant beaches express a collision of
temperaments, terrible for both and disastrous in its results,
but without solution, meaning, or ultimate profit. Hence in
Euripides' world people seem less agents than acted on, less
in command than commanded by impulses or forces greater
than themselves. The illumination of the middle and late fifth
century had much enlarged men's view of the world: Herodotus described distant peoples, Anaxagoras and Democritus
speculated on atoms, Meton's new calendar displaced gods
from the sky, and the author of the tract *On the Sacred Disease* (epilepsy) called all diseases equally natural. But the par-
adoxical result of these splendid acts of inquiry was that human beings bulked less large in the scheme of things; for all
his intellectuality, Euripides was less respectful of the human
race than Sophocles, and infinitely less so than Aeschylus.
Hippolytus and Phaedra come near being pawns, if not of
actual goddesses, at least of impulses and temperaments that
are as powerful.

  After Hippolytus has seen the statues of the two goddesses
and has rejected the one and greeted the other as his invisible
companion in the secret wilds and untouched hills, Phaedra
is presented as delirious and near death. She has found no
means to keep her good name and conceal her passion for her
stepson except suicide by starvation, but in her delirium she

thinks that she is following him on the hills and sands. On recovering sanity, she tells the women of the chorus in a famous speech that she has often brooded at night on why life goes wrong: not through the nature of the human mind, she says, since many people are intelligent, but because we do not do the things that we know we should, being distracted by idleness, pleasure, talk, the bright bane of leisure, and by what she cryptically calls the bad form of self-respect, which seems to be an excessive regard for appearances.[7] The speech, which has a close parallel in the *Medea*,[8] is striking because it expresses doubt of that very illumination that Euripides himself felt and that marked the age. Socrates held that because evil makes a man worse, no one willingly commits it; hence if one does so, it must be through ignorance; hence knowledge is goodness.[9] Thucydides, too, in tracing the decisions of the war as a guide to future statesmen, tacitly assumes that correct judgment produces success; affairs to him are analyzable, and everything hinges on the right use of intelligence. Sophocles' Oedipus, who in answering the riddle of the sphinx had been the very prototype of the saving intellect, had remained characterized by a certain thrusting restlessness, a tone or aura of uncertainty, deeply and mysteriously gripping in Sophocles' portrayal; it proves to emanate from himself and not from circumstances, hence leads him ultimately back to knowledge of himself. But Phaedra's speech goes farther and is the more disquieting because it fits the action, and not of this play only. Euripides' idealistic characters are often, like Hippolytus, young people who have not yet felt the wear of experience;[10] older people, who know more of the world,

commonly represent its or nature's ways as powerful and beyond resisting. Phaedra's nurse now does so, asserting that
Aphrodite is a great goddess who sways every species of creatures and overrides all resistance.[11] She finally extorts Hippolytus's name from Phaedra as the object of her passion, but
on approaching him is met by vituperation as violent as the
queen's love; he and Phaedra are equally in the grip of emotions as opposite as the two goddesses, but unlike the problems pursued by Socrates and Thucydides and even by Oedipus, these emotions are beyond reason. The queen saves her
name by suicide, but true to herself even then, she vengefully
and falsely accuses Hippolytus to her returning husband Theseus. Theseus accepts no defense from the young man and
banishes him, pronouncing a curse given him by his father,
Poseidon. The curse is fulfilled: a wild bull emerging from
the sea terrifies Hippolytus's horses and wrecks his chariot on
the beaches where he had loved to drive. Though Artemis
appears to him as he lies dying and makes clear his innocence to Theseus, she leaves before his death, and among the
many dark lines of the play, none is bleaker than his parting
comment to her: "You lightly end our long association."[12]
The bull that destroyed Hippolytus has the violence that he
would have excluded from his beautiful world. Aphrodite
proves to be the powerful goddess that the nurse declared
her, but knowledge of the fact does not alter the result, and
intelligence has clarified the world only to find itself power-
less before the world's contingencies.

Nineteen of Euripides' plays survive, and partly for this
reason, partly because his mood veered much more impres-

sionably than Sophocles', it is harder to keep a clear track in
following him. By bringing to the stage such women as Phaedra and Medea, he broached new spheres of private feeling,
and as the war advanced he saw it as having its most brutal
effect on women. In his *Andromache, Hecuba,* and *Trojan
Women* the story of Troy expresses quite simply the violence
of men to women, conquerors to conquered, and strong to
weak. Yet during the first decade of the war he championed
the enlightenment of Athens as against the oligarchic rigor
and secrecy of Sparta and Thebes, and one admires the logic
of a mind which, finding private life entangled in emotion,
sought remedy in the vision of public reason and order. The
fullest statement of this social faith is in *The Suppliants,*
where Theseus defends the democratic energy and humanity
of Athens in something like the tones of Pericles; but the
finest statement is a brief ode of the *Medea,* produced in the
spring of 431 on the eve of the war, which memorably expresses the brightness of Athens before the shadow. Theoretical even there and alluding to current ideas on climate and
civilization which elsewhere appear in the Hippocratic tract
Airs, Waters, and Places, he sees in the bright skies and tempered winds and water of Attica persuasions to harmony of
spirit; Aphrodite breathes gentle airs and, wreathing roses in
her hair, makes love and wisdom partners, joint creators of
excellence.[13] The Greek union of emotion and reason finds no
finer words. But this public faith darkened as the war dragged
on, and it is an act of purest intuition that just in the years of
the crowning Athenian disaster at Syracuse, he turned in the
Ion, the *Iphigenia in Tauris,* and the *Helena* to lonely themes

of reconciliation in distant places. These plays correspond in date to Aristophanes' *Birds* and share its fugitive mood. Euripides is surely not saying that loss and search always end in reunion; it is rather that the wide world, not the city, is the heart's trackless dimension, in which people are cast on themselves and from doubt and wandering find unforeseen arrivals. Outer travel becomes the setting of inner travel, but if the mood is somewhat that of the *Odyssey,* the travelers are less able and confident than Odysseus, and the world less viable to purpose. The width of things and the isolation of the characters look forward to much in the Hellenistic Age, and even in the *Aeneid,* rather than back to the sureness of the *Odyssey.* Of the classical Greek writers, Euripides notably created a language for privacy of experience, and he paradoxically did so by pressing intellectuality farther than other poets and finding no solution in it.

He left Athens for Macedon in his last years, presumably in disillusion, and his greatest play, the mysterious *Bacchae,* was posthumously produced not long before the occupation of the city by the Spartans in the autumn of 404. Little survives of Aeschylus's three trilogies on the power of the god of wine, inspiration, and freedom; Sophocles characteristically seems not to have found these myths congenial; and one lacks tradition in trying to judge this play. At first glance it resembles the *Hippolytus*: in destroying the rigid Pentheus, who would forbid the new god from Thebes and keep women from following him as Maenads to the mountains, Dionysus shows an emotional force analogous to Aphrodite's. From this standpoint, the play states most centrally and at the end of his life Euripides' abiding view of emotion as the blind force that drives the world. Several descriptions convey the young god's flowing hair and laughing ease, and odes describe green glades in the mountains where the Maenads run without effort, sleep smilingly, and drink milk that gushes from the earth; everything about Dionysus speaks of natural growth, and he lives, so to speak, in a world of curves and ellipses as of leaves, tendrils, grapevines, and animals. The urban and moralistic Pentheus, by contrast, suggests the straight lines and sharp angles of inhibiting thought, and in resisting Dionysus he vainly tries to reduce the endless burgeoning and novelty of life to plan and rule. Such a view of the play may be essentially correct, but Pentheus is also more subtly susceptible to Dionysus than Hippolytus was to Aphrodite, and in a terrible scene the god breaks down the king's resistance, has him put on women's clothes, and leads him through his own prurient curiosity to meet his death spying on the Maenads.[14]

Now, if the Trojan myths evidently conveyed to Euripides the oppression of the weak by the strong and of women by men, the Theban myths seem to have held for him quite another class of associations, having to do with the grip of the past on the present (a theme of the just earlier *Phoenissae*), with retention, pride, tightness, and fear of freedom. These ideas also certainly color the play. Pentheus's mother Agaue, who kills her son in bacchic delusion thinking him an animal, was introduced at the start as doubting that Dionysus was the son by Zeus of her sister Semele. If Pentheus conveys the rigidity inherited from the past, she conveys its pride, and Dionysus, who is both winning and cruel, may be thought forced to cruelty by their insistence. In this view the past through habit and limitedness builds dikes against change; fear and self-repression add further motive, and the most established people are the most rigid. The chorus of Maenads praises the life of common people over that of the fastidious and intellectual; the god, they say, approves those who "in sunlight and fond nights find happiness and wisely keep mind and heart from pretentious men. What the vulgar mass approves and does would I accept."[15] These opinions are the chorus's and need not be the poet's, and yet the play concerns a yielding to life as something greater and more renewing than fixed forms and inherited positions. Such a view of the play as directed against rigidity and of Dionysus as the god of renewal may be not so far after all from the *Hippolytus,* in which both the young hero and Phaedra fastidiously want to live with sure elegance and to prescribe, so to speak, the conditions of a beautiful existence. But however one tries to understand the continuity, it obviously exists not only between these two plays but through all the plays, in an outlook intuitively sensitive to emergent ideas and unforeseen actualities. The wholeness of Sophocles' mythic vision has yielded in Euripides to something that is both bigger and more broken: bigger in his sense of the power and size of the world and its way of forcing the mind to see it in new, usually undesired ways; more broken in his characters' inability—which is perhaps to say his own inability—to hold it in control. Yet honesty, including intellectual honesty, takes many forms, some of which approximate courage, and high among these is the power to stare reality in the face. Such directness of

gaze yields a kind of control, if not in the sense of a Sophoclean dignity and integrity, yet in the authority that derives
from holding nothing back, from using all powers to grasp
how things stand even at their most unpleasant. It is this kind
of control that Euripides not only has but first conceived it
possible to have.

With Thucydides we approach the logical end of these lectures, not in the sense that like the philosophers and orators
of the next century he laid the foundation of our analytical
world and created the prose styles to express it, but because
he was the first extant writer who in a thoroughgoing way
thought analytically. If the works of Protagoras and Democritus had survived, we should probably class these men with
him, and Socrates of course belongs in the company, though
we catch only his reflected light. Some medical tracts, including the *Epidemics, Prognostic,* and *Regimen in Acute Diseases,* which are attributed to Hippocrates himself, antedate
Thucydides' history; hence they may deserve the title of our
first works of analytical prose, and the Tetralogies of the ora-
tor Antiphon and the so-called Old Oligarch's *Constitution
of Athens* also claim a place. But in sheer magnitude both of
idea and of application the History overshadows all these;
and though, like geologists contemplating an old range, we
may imagine a once massive upthrust and infer the emergence of many peaks, yet in the worn range that we see the
History stands central. It did not do so at the time, presumably because, as the general who had lost Athens' Thracian
territory to the Spartan Brasidas in 424, Thucydides was ex-
iled for the remaining twenty years of the war, to the benefit

of his History—since, as he says,[16] he was then able to follow both sides—but at the cost of notability at home. Xenophon among others completed his unfinished work, but Plato and Aristotle seem unaware of him; of extant fourth-century writers only Isocrates knows him well. Exile surely does more than enforce acquaintance with new scenes, and it might not be profitless to trace similarities of outlook in Thucydides, Dante, Machiavelli, Turgenev, and, if blindness be a form of exile, Milton. Reflection on formerly vivid but now lost experience must, one imagines, cause a man to see certain people and events more sharply, and if he has a schematic mind, to make them representative of classes and kinds of motives and outcomes, with the result that his diagnostic turn of mind grows on him and he increasingly sees in events the functioning of an interworking structure. Such a mental structure may be an exile's main reality; he has been wrenched from nearly everything else. If so, exile enhanced in Thucydides the analytical bent that he formed from youth on in Athens, and accident intensified what he shared with his generation. The British philosopher of history R. G. Collingwood[17] called Thucydides the father of the social sciences, Herodotus the father of history, because Thucydides saw things as aspects of a process whereas Herodotus saw them as springing from specific events. The distinction may fade on reflection, since historians must choose between millions of past events and must emphasize some while neglecting far the greater number, evidently on the conscious or unconscious assumption that these few events somehow dominate or embrace the others. If Thucydides found Herodotus superficial and incomplete, as he clearly did, it is because he thought that he himself had penetrated to deeper stages of causality and interworking. This is only to say again that he pressed analysis much farther. He saw the war as exemplifying clashes that would continue to occur between and within states, hence sprang from the nature of political life, and he expressly wrote for future readers who might apply the teachings of the past to their present.[18]

Our first assumption that eye and mind jointly report reality should perhaps give way, as the Greek world grew more complex, to Buffon's familiar dictum "Le styl c'est l'homme même"—possibly in the altered form "Le styl c'est l'âge." At least, as theory emerges, it makes new marriages with style, and as visible people and objects prescribed Homer's reality, so did the shape of sentences prescribe Thucydides'. In its first effort to find a mature form, prose did not instantly rise from simple independent statements to the periodic structures which, elaborated by Isocrates and Demosthenes, were to pass to Cicero and from him to the cadences of Gibbon and Burke. The so-called antithetical style intervened as the first stage of consciously ambitious prose. It must have been the sophists' great novelty in the later fifth century; as such, it is reflected in the debates of Euripides' plays. Indeed, it marks a generation that saw things by paired opposites, in speeches, paragraphs, sentences, clauses. Thucydides is beyond compare the master of this style, and though one dwells on it chiefly as a key to his thought, its pervasive tone of excitement is worth noting. It stands midway between the two poles of the simple and the periodic styles. As we noted of Homer, when Hector sets his shining helmet on the ground, the one statement, matching the one action, reflects a mind that sees each thing for itself; the periodic style, by contrast, subordinates thoughts and impressions to a ruling idea which gives unity to the sentence and around which all else revolves in fit degrees of subordination. The main clause is king; the other parts of the sentence have become his somewhat sapless courtiers. But in the antithetical style a ceaseless struggle goes on between these opposite impulses toward things and toward the ruling idea. Thought has sufficiently emerged so that no thing or idea stands alone in its own statement, but each perpetually confronts and, so to speak, rubs against some opposite; yet because these opposites remain individually so vivid, the central idea, far from dominating, can hardly contain them, and a sentence becomes a kind of boxing ring, often for several pairs of antagonists—not so much dominating as simply marking off the encounter. "War," writes Thucydides in a famous chapter on revolutions, "by removing the security of daily life is a violent teacher and levels the moods of the masses to their circumstances. Cities accordingly turned factional, and those that lagged carried further by report from elsewhere their extravagance in innovation of attack and singularity of reprisal. People changed in usage the normal relationship of words to deeds: insane daring was judged loyal courage, cautious delay was called specious fear, temperance the mask of cowardice, and general intelligence general futility. Frenetic suddenness was explained by our human condition, and plotting by safety as a polite pretext for self-protection. A violent man was always credible, his opponent suspect."[19] One could go on at length, but even these sentences may make the main point: namely, that by antithesis each member of a pair has such tension toward the other that even when both are abstract words, they breathe an almost human aliveness. Ideas and human beings are never far apart in Thucydides, and the reason is that he sees ideas struggling with each other in human fashion. In this first stage of conscious Greek intellectuality he brings to theory the vitality of action.

It follows that his view of the war and his design for the History fall into antitheses. In essence these are two: the contrast of Athens with Sparta, and the contrast of the Athens of Pericles with the Athens of his successors. What has been said so far about the change of Athens into a metropolis sets the tone of the former contrast: Sparta is a land power, agricultural, oligarchic, traditional in habit and outlook, loath to jeopardize her control of helots at home or her long-held priority abroad; Athens is a sea power, mercantile, democratic, recently risen through the energy that is the fruit of freedom to a position that endangers Sparta's ancient hegemony. The two antagonists enter the war at the head of leagues, and the example that Thucydides sees for posterity is of a world that has partly merged national states into bigger spheres, yet has missed the final step toward unity—a world, moreover, that was divided between settled and rising states, between traditional and novel forms of government, and, not least important, between simpler and more complex economies. The war is not at bottom an encounter between two states but a struggle for direction and unity within a civilization. As the History advances, Athens' true antagonist proves to be not

Sparta but herself. To Thucydides, Athens' naval power not only expresses a far richer and more complex economy, but also, being fitly joined with a democratic constitution, elicits an energy and openness that amount to a new stage of civilization. Sparta's long dominance had been achieved by heavily armed infantry, the so-called hoplites, who, since most Greek cities depended on local grain, could force the choice of battle or starvation. But Athens by her long walls and command of the sea had outflown this dilemma. The contrast then becomes one between a sea-culture and a land-culture: the former unregimented, versatile, skeptical, inventive; the other disciplined, traditional, and relatively immobile. The crux lies within the sea-mind itself—whether, with all its vigor, it will remain sufficiently restrained in policy and constant in leadership—and it is this question that sets the second antithesis, between Pericles and his successors. As we have noted, Thucydides seems to have been a young man, perhaps in his middle twenties, at the outbreak of the war in 431, and being connected with one of the chief conservative families, he was apparently drawn to Pericles by a kind of intellectual conversion. Greek opinion, he says, expected Sparta to win easily because she always had,[20] but the young future historian evidently accepted Pericles' belief that Athens had put herself beyond Sparta's attack and would win if for the present she simply sought equality with Sparta, not further conquest. Of the three speeches of Pericles that he reports, the famous Funeral Oration takes added luster as our sole full statement of democratic theory from the great period. As noted earlier, it is a paradox that the Athenians who invented democracy left their chief record of it in the later works of Plato and others, works written retrospectively in the troubled period after the defeat. "We love beauty with simplicity and pursue wisdom without softness," said Pericles,[21] and the words convey an ideal of taste unhedged by privilege and of intelligence unclouded by suspicion. Athenians, he goes on, reach policies by open debate and believe bravery to consist not in ignorance but in facing dangers consciously undertaken. Imperfect as any actual democracy, the Athenian included, may be, this is democracy's first and perhaps its clearest statement, unrivaled in grasp of that individual self-respect, mental and moral, which democracy fosters and which makes it work.

Yet not even the intellectual Pericles foresaw the plague that would attend the crowding of the city in the face of the first Spartan invasion. He himself died of it, and there may be no sharper contrast in literature than that between the lucent reason of Pericles' speeches and the city's helplessness before the epidemic. As we noted, Sophocles' *Oedipus Tyrannus* seems to have been written in these years; and though Oedipus as a character is himself and not Pericles, yet intellectual courage before the unknown remains among the final achievements of Periclean Athens. His successors, says Thucydides, being more on a level with one another, courted the demos for their personal gain; hence they led Athens to adventures which, when successful, aggrandized the leaders but when unsuccessful imperiled the city.[22] The rest of the History recounts the mounting series of these adventures. Pericles' estimate of Athenian strength and of the naval policy by which it showed itself was proved right in the victory of

Pylos and the ensuing Spartan overtures for peace,[23] but even that strength did not survive Alcibiades' plan of reducing Sicily by taking its chief city, Syracuse. The series of mistakes in that campaign, including the exile of Alcibiades himself, culminated in total disaster. Brutalizing hardship caused the mood of faction and civil war described in the passage quoted earlier to sweep Greece, and Athens was not immune. When nine years after Syracuse and seven years after the end of Thucydides' unfinished History the Spartans occupied Athens and set up the repressive rule of their supporters, the city succumbed less to its enemies than to its own factiousness. Dark as this outcome is, and divided as the democracy finally proved to be, one may reflect that the government emanated from first to last quite simply from town meetings. So impressive a structure has rarely rested on so exposed a base, and the marvel is less that its policy swayed dangerously under heavy strain than that it stayed relatively constant for more than a century. The exalted doctrine of the Funeral Oration is not proved wrong by the outcome.

"Lack of the mythical," Thucydides wrote in the famous chapter on his method, "may rob my work of charm. But if those find it useful who will wish to scan the exact character of past events—events that by reason of human nature will recur in like or analogous form—that will suffice. It has been written not for a day's hearing but as a possession forever."[24] Here seems to speak the confident voice of rationalism: a scorn of pleasure in mere stories (perhaps Herodotus's but also stories generally); the assumption that events illustrate some guiding scheme which intelligence can grasp and which, human nature being constant, will recur; and—in the idea of usefulness—the belief that this knowledge may be acted on. The sophist Protagoras in Plato's dialogue expresses a like confidence that he knows and can teach the political art.[25] Further, early oratory relied on a doctrine of likelihood that posited constancy in human nature—the young acting like the young, the old like the old, democrats like democrats, oligarchs like oligarchs—a constancy that made the future more or less predictable. Medicine notably sought predictability—as we have seen, the *Prognostic* is thought a Hippocratic work—and it is not too much to call this belief in characteristic and foreseeable stages of disease one of the two chief Hippocratic tenets, the other being rigor of observation. As is clear from Thucydides' account of the plague, he knew some medicine, and he evidently thought that just as the human body in disease shows clear stages of crisis, so also does the body politic. He at least bends medical terms to the use of history; and more important, he values in statesmen, notably in Themistocles and Pericles, the power of foresight.[26] The sentence just quoted makes clear that he wishes to enhance this power in future readers; as with the Hippocratics, a precondition of his doing so will be his correctness of observation. It is part of his huge originality to have pressed the sophistic doctrine of likelihood to a quasi-medical rigor, or, conversely, to have stretched the prognostic aims of medicine to include the state itself. The new rationalism, he surely felt, had put into his hand the true key to history: not to history as dead and finished, but to the living course of events, which analysis might help a man control.

Yet to try to press this confidence to clear conclusions is somewhere to lose the track. That, in his view, states exert power in their own interest,[27] that democracy released in Athens a fresh stage of creativity,[28] that sea-power roused and accompanied a mercantile economy which spurred the individual and vastly strengthened the state,[29] that history showed and will show successive peoples rising to power through the will to do and right judgment of possibilities[30]—all this is clear enough. But what were the limits to Athens' possible power? Pericles warned against expansion during the war,[31] and the people's neglect of this warning in hope of "a perpetual source of employment"[32] in a wider empire seemed to Thucydides a chief cause of the defeat. But was this quietism of Pericles only temporary, to be reversed when Sparta's outdated power had faded still further, or did he at bottom question the restraint of that very energy that had carried Athens to the height? Again, the Athenians' statement at the parley before the outbreak that ability and will in themselves justify power differs sharply in tone from the naked assertion of Athenian power against the weak Melians.[33] Thucydides seems to have approved of the one and disapproved of the other, but what differentiates the two cases? If only the strength or weakness of an opponent, the standard is virtually that of Homeric glory. Further, intelligence that correctly gauges reality is praised, but hope that falsifies it is scorned. Yet temperance is needed to restrain dangerous hopes —the kind of temperance that is praised in the virtuous but incompetent Nicias—whereas Alcibiades, who in Thucydides' judgment might have brought off victory at Syracuse, supported the expedition through self-interest in order to pay his debts, though it flew in the face of Pericles' warning.[34] Where in practice is the line to be drawn between shrewd estimate and dangerous hope? Pericles, it is said, ascribed to himself four merits; he saw what was necessary, he could expound it, he was patriotic, and he was above money.[35] It was Athens' misfortune that no one after his death combined these virtues; Alcibiades had the former two, Nicias the latter two. But once war has inflamed a people and the factionalism described in the previously quoted passage has advanced, where lies assurance that these happily combined attributes will survive? If it seems clear that the downward spiral of war should have been checked and an early peace made—which was surely the historian's view, since he thought that the Spartan overtures of 425 after Pylos should have been accepted[36]—how does this fear of a long war comport with the view of Athens' great inherent power? And how under the democracy, the source of her power, were emotions, the source of her errors, to be kept in check? Finally, such questions rouse a more fundamental doubt: namely, though understanding of political forces implies the power to control them, their character as forces implies necessity. For all his rational optimism, Thucydides leaves no stronger impression than of the iron consequences of even a single error. Matchless as is his perception of issues, his gripping power lies also in the sheer urgency with which events unroll. This sense of ineluctability is in obvious conflict with his belief in reasoned choice. Though he gazed less fixedly than Euripides on this dark truth, its chilling presence as strongly molds his work. Much of both men's power lies in their pursuing reason to the vision of its opposite.

Chapter Four

THE RATIONAL MIND

The mood that dawned on Athens in the eighty-odd years from the end of the Peloponnesian War in 404 to the deaths of Alexander and Aristotle in 323 and 322 created a new world, in itself and prospectively. It is often vaguely said that the modern West reflects its Greek origins; if so, the mold was set in the individualism, the speculation, the ease, the humanity, that mark these years. Not that decisive origins do not go back farther: Homer's sparkling clarities, the god-touched visions of Aeschylus and Pindar, at nearer range the stringencies of Euripides and Thucydides all leave their residue. But in the fourth century it is as if the early mist had risen to uncover no longer a world of gods but a bright mid-morning—no narrow scene, since philosophers, professing themselves such and organized in schools for speculation, explore its nature and horizons, nevertheless a brisk and busy scene, which speech-writers manipulate and comic poets mirror. There are fashions in scholarship, and this sunlit tangibility of the fourth century, doubtless from its lack of shadow, now rouses less enthusiasm than do eras nearer the dawn. We have in fact made many of its creations our own, though largely indirectly through its effect on Augustan Rome and the latter's on the European and English Enlightenment. Distinction in scope and style between prose and verse, and the use of high and low styles within each; the presence side by side of polite public norms and bold academic speculations; grace of statuary and architecture; interest in money and the prerequisites of a decent life, yet acceptance of time, change, and luck; an eye for motive and character, yet awareness of their malleability by institutions—these and much else describe a world that we take for granted and even protest against. One evident difference exists; it would not have occurred to Plato or Isocrates to admire primitive Cycladic statues of the late third millennium B.C. or the gold face-masks that Schliemann unearthed from the Mycenaean shaft-graves. To the men of the fourth century the forms of rational order represented an achieved triumph; to us they can seem trite. The fourth century expresses form and summation, and since all springs imply summers and youth the commitments of middle life, we may admire this great age which transmitted while it fulfilled.

Clearly no single cause suffices to explain so wide a change. The twenty-seven years of the Peloponnesian War—nearly a generation—constitute what Aristotle might have judged the efficient cause. The war brought losses of men and money, loss of empire (though Athens soon regained some of her old naval ascendancy), loss of confidence in the promises of leaders, awareness that the state could fall apart into conflicting interests and at best hardly contained them, and—subtlest loss—surfeit of the former dream of conquest. In Aristophanes' *Knights,* produced in the eighth year of the war, the demagogue had pointed from the Pnyx to Caria and Carthage as if they shimmered at the horizon; in Thucydides' description of the departure of the fleet for Syracuse, libations are poured from gold and silver urns, and the crews in high spirits race as far as Aegina.[1] The sea seemed a smiling goddess, and Pericles' reasoned acceptance of war sprang even in him, much more so in the mass of the people, from sheer disbelief that Athenian ships could ever lose. In Greek thought democracy is connected with the sea, poetically in Aeschylus's sweeping reaches, politically and strategically in Thucydides. It was this sparkling invitation that now vanished; the old faith that unity at home would always back the ships, much as they in turn could catch at sea the glint of Athena's spear from the Acropolis, had proved delusive. There is little about the sea in fourth-century literature: Plato distrusts it and would build his ideal city well inland remote from its fickleness; in the comic fragments it supplies the fish markets. The buoyancy that has swept many peoples into dreams of expansion and conquest, only to evaporate as suddenly as it had come, is one of the enigmas of history. "If—since all things by nature decline—we even now may some day suffer defeat," says Pericles of the Athenian power, "yet memory of it will last forever,... and though the quietist may criticize, he who again feels the will to do will emulate it."[2] In the fifth century the sea had been Athens' bright avenue not only to space in the world but to space of hope and creativity, and beneath all the lucid creations of the age is an element of pure exhilaration. Art is an act of being before it is an act of thought, and the soaring adornments of the Acropolis first of all express pride of life. To pass beyond the end of the great period is to see it for what it was, a moment of invitation when the world seemed open.

But at least two other main forces abetted the change: the thoroughgoing victory of what was earlier termed a conceptual way of thought over the old mythological way, and the rise of something like an urban middle class. Poets can deceive, as the Greeks themselves often said, and their early prominence may weigh too much with us; for centuries they alone had voice, and their world still seems full of gods and heroes. If ordinary people felt otherwise, their mute emotions survive only in the inferences of historians and archeologists. Yet the poets in fact flourished, hence must have answered an existent mood. Listeners who heard Homer can only have recognized in his oral art and heroic themes the perfection of what they themselves had sometimes attempted or at least had known since childhood; as we have seen, such admiration must even explain the writing down of his poems, which were conceived orally. Similarly, the crowds that heard Aeschylus in the early theater surely echoed his grandiloquence; they too had been reared on songs and dances. Whether or not a man could read, he was moved by language and an acute judge of it—indeed, the less literate a man was, the more acutely he must have heard, since the poet's language alone lent him flight and scope. We pursued this question earlier in trying to imagine the mood of the great poetic age. But the spread of writing gradually created another outlook;

Socrates in the *Apology* speaks of books for sale in the marketplace,[3] and Euripides reputedly had a library. Life became more diverse, more complicated, allowed more individuality, let people work out more fully their own tastes; new techniques grew fast, both the specialized kinds such as show in the medical tracts or the mathematical references of Plato's *Theaetetus,* and the more general competence that Isocrates held to be the aim of education. A successful man mastered some of these; he would think that he had less to learn from the old poetic themes than, say, from Xenophon's tract on state revenue or on running a farm; in Aristophanes' *Birds* a character who recites Pindar is absurd.[4] Plato of course held higher aims for prose: nothing less than his faith in human rationality and in the mind's power to guide itself through dialectic, on which view the old poetry was actively misleading.

But most people's motives were simpler; they chiefly wanted to better themselves, and it is this impulse that prompted the previous statement about the rise of a middle class. The heroic outlook that blazed in Homer, took brilliant new forms in Pindar and Aeschylus, and reached lapidary definition in Sophocles, was aristocratic, if not in the later European sense of rank and title, yet in the sense that minor success and daily comfort were no fitting test of a man's self-fidelity. It is part of the greatness of the fourth century that this temper, though with new substance and emphasis, descended in the example of Socrates. But the democracy to which Plato objected on the ground that, like a bazaar,[5] it catered to all wants, was at odds with the old personal heroism, and the disenchantment of defeat clouded the corporate heroism that had flashed in the great war. Later analogies disarm criticism. Expansive eras open opportunities in which many wish to share; the society grows more diffused; though sharing is wider, daily life is not spared striving, gossip, mutual oversight, and the usual human responses to success and failure. A desire for reasonable decency sets the tone, and the wider norm is necessarily nearer the middle. This is the background to Plato's flights of theory and Aristotle's learning. But as with most things Greek, it emerges for the first time, and though history will repeat this evaporation of the heroic into the quotidian, the discovery that there can be grace in small events, that simple prose has charms that grand verse lacks, that lightness, wit, purity of line, and an unpressing manner have their place in life, was the discovery of this age. If Plato created the language of philosophy, many joined to create the language of decent grace, and it is hard to know which was to have the greater influence.

To begin with this light, quotidian side, ancient rhetoric— itself an invention of the age, though from origins in the fifth-century sophists—distinguished between ornate and plain styles. Cicero, for example, would one day judge his own manner a happy mean between Hortensius's floridity and Caesar's spareness; but needless to say Cicero's self-estimate was not always shared, and others would judge Caesar's manner not spare but Attic. The first sentences of Plato's *Republic* illustrate the new naturalness: "I went down yesterday to the Piraeus with Glaucon, Ariston's son, to say my prayers to the goddess and also because I wanted to see how they would conduct the ceremony, this being the first time. The local people's procession struck me as in fact beautiful, though the Thracians' seemed less fitting. So after saying our prayers and looking on we were on our way up to town, when Polemarchus, Cephalus's son, from a distance caught sight of us homeward bound and had his slave run and ask us to wait for him. He took hold of my cloak from behind saying, 'Polemarchus asks you to wait.' When I turned and asked where he was, 'There,' he answered, 'coming along after you. Do wait.' 'By all means,' said Glaucon, 'we will.'" Plato has other manners, too, but that he chose to begin his chief work in just this way tells something of him and of the age. The Greeks, to be sure, had never wholly yielded to greatness and distance and nobility; the opening of the *Odyssey* shows Telemachus in the graceful light of home and first travel, and Odysseus himself finds final contentment in familiar Ithaca. Attic vases sometimes show two scenes, one from mythology (say, Theseus and the Marathonian boar) and the other from daily life (say, young men with a discus and javelin and elders looking on)—so in the culture as a whole the common gives margin to the great. But proportions change between the two sides, and if Pericles in the Funeral Oration had held that in Athens beauty could be simple and pleasure in it the antidote to dullness,[6] still it is only now that the lesson is fully learned.

One may set as a boundary on the other side the deepening violence and insecurity of third- and second-century Greece described by Polybius. In all his huge work he mentions Homer only a few times, Pindar and Euripides only once or twice; in effect he omits the poets and philosophers; in one memorable passage he mentions village songs and dances in Arcadia, but simply as useful for implanting restraint.[7] The Macedonian dominance, intervention by the other Hellenistic powers, the Gauls' and the Aetolians' raiding and looting, the recrudescence of tyranny and the frequent fighting between the cities—this violent course of events had so reduced his expectations that all that he tacitly asks is a basic order. The fourth century can thus seem a kind of island—an interval when there was wealth enough, when daily decencies were sufficiently widespread to afford many people pleasure, and when some had leisure for a life of theory. One may not of course properly speak of the contentment of an age; only individuals attain contentment. For the society at large outer events continually intrude and resources are never adequate; thus Demosthenes now rises to the menace of Macedon and Isocrates urges the exploitation of Persia. Theory, further, is adventure beyond the present, and Plato, Aristotle, and their schools embark on this new odyssey, though one may add that the former finds final repose in the ideal forms, the latter in the philosopher's act of contemplation. Nevertheless, even to see, if not to be able to hold and keep, the level beauty of common life is not so frequent an attainment that it may be looked down on. The new language for the grace of the ordinary is in its unobtrusive way a major creation.

A few more examples will suffice. From the famous march in winter through the mountains of Armenia to the Black Sea, Xenophon remembered among much else a hot spring smoking in a valley from ground bare of snow. Some of his men refused to go on, telling him to kill them if he wished, they would not move; but he and others soon reached a village consisting of dwellings dug into the hillside and companionably occupied by livestock. A wedding celebration for the chief's daughter was going on, now in its eighth day; they were hospitably received, and the frostbitten men at the spring were brought on. There were bowls of barley wine with kernels floating on top, and people would be dragged with much hilarity to drink through straws, which he notes lacked what he called knees. True to their habits, the Greeks thought that crowns would be fitting but had only hay to make them from. A charming touch is that the bridegroom was absent; he had gone out rabbit-hunting.[8] Would an account so full of authentic details have been made earlier? A chorus in Aristophanes' *Acharnians* describes a fish-fry in a village with the flames flying and a Thracian sauce heating up, and in the *Peace* the tettix sings while the farmer surveys his grapevines, eats a fig, talks of the good weather, rubs thyme in his fingers, and mixes himself a drink.[9] Such passages are among the enchantments of Aristophanes, but Xenophon's tone is more factual, not as a background to flights of imagination but as actuality. Again, earlier in the narrative, after the death of Cyrus at Cunaxa and the murder of the Greek generals by his defecting supporter Tissaphernes, Xenophon summarizes the character of the tough Spartan disciplinarian Clearchus, the Boeotian Proxenus, honorable but unable to control his troops, and the Thessalian Meno (the same who gives his name to the Platonic dialogue), whom he disliked and distrusted.[10] These are appraisals of unique men, sharply drawn from an exact memory, and they share the sense of temperament and personality that marks the early Platonic dialogues before the *Republic*: for example, the opening of the *Protagoras*. In this delightful scene young Hippocrates wakes Socrates with the excited news that the great sophist is in town, then guides him to Callias's house, where a whole troop of sophists is gathered.[11] Protagoras walks up and down attended by a following that is careful to wheel and fall in behind him when he turns; the sickly Prodicus is still in his room lying down; Hippias, an older man who professes a mass of somewhat unrelated information, sits jealously removed from Protagoras answering astronomical questions. The intention is satirical but the characters emerge sharply, as in a serious spirit do all the participants in the *Phaedo,* even the humble jailer, in the closing scene of Socrates' death. To be sure, a fragment by Ion of Chios about Sophocles at a dinner party survives from the fifth century, but it is exceptional and Ion was not an Athenian.[12] What is new in these examples is their confinement to unique, yet not extraordinary, events, as if whatever else life might offer, it gave first of all this daily clarity. To borrow architectural terms, the tone is Ionic, not Doric, and purity of idiom imparts a grace and naturalness that have the effect of light.

Time has not been kind to the so-called middle and new comedy, which, unlike tragedy, greatly flourished. We noted in Euripides' late romantic plays of search and travel—the *Iphigenia in Tauris, Helena,* and *Ion*—a new voice of individualism, as of people surprised by accident and misfortune and sometimes wresting unforeseen gains from them. He had his chief influence on this later comedy, and not in plot and spirit only but in the light language that he helped create. Many fragments of this comedy survive, partly because of the quotability of its tolerant comments on the human scene, partly because Athenaeus, author about A.D. 200 of a huge tract, *The Deipnosophists,* on dining and its perquisites, found in these plays innumerable mention of wine, drinking vessels, meats, sauces, fruits, vegetables, breads, cakes, and above all fish, the food that the Athenians most esteemed. To think that Poseidon had come to this! Athenaeus colors these plays with the impression of an endless meal, but there was obviously a good deal of eating, or at least of thought and talk about eating. But to omit this subject and to choose virtually at random among writers and fragments, Alexis, Menander's uncle, born in Thurii, whose long life and over two hundred plays spanned the later decades of the century, speaks of the poor outliving the rich; of late guests spoiling the skill of cooks; of jokes producing anger and anger blows; of life as a journey to a brief festival from the realms of shadow and death; of sleep as neither god nor mortal, always new, always lost, invisible but known to everyone; of lovers as resembling soldiers and equally needing stratagems and courage in adversity; of a good posture as an adornment to a man and pleasant to look at; of the mystery why long hair, which we naturally have, is irritating; of men who dine alone and poets who dislike music as being only half alive; of husbands who are dominated at home as resembling the disenfranchised who are debarred from public office.[13] These examples, if doubtless too random, serve at least to illustrate the new scope. Put them beside Plato and a mood appears that can embrace the most and the least trivial, that accepts the daily with the distant and acknowledges the claims of each—that in short has discovered tolerance, and what is more, a language for its variety. This is the mood that was indirectly transmitted to the eighteenth-century essayists and thence onward, the mood and style of catholicity. Menander's *Dyscolus, Ill-Tempered Man,* first published from papyrus in 1958, happily at last provides a complete play; it seems to have been produced in 317, five years after Aristotle's death.[14] If its romantic plot and limpid Greek go back to Euripides, its theme of the renewal of the city by the country is in Aristophanes' spirit, but lighter, much less robust, done with a smile. A politely bred youth accidentally precedes his family to a picnic at a shrine of Pan and the Nymphs. He is pursuing the pretty daughter of a flinty and half-deranged farmer who lives nearby; tries in his unpracticed way to gain favor with the tough old man; gets blisters, ruins his city clothes, but helps pull the farmer out of a well. Needless to say, he ends by getting the girl, and—what may prove as important to him—by being introduced, so to speak, to the country god Pan. The girl's hard-pressed brother, some city-bred servants, the usual busy and complaining cook, the hero's demanding mother, and his tolerant, well-to-do father set off the obduracy of the central figure, who nevertheless shows the rock whence they were all hewn. In Theocritus's wonderful Seventh Idyl the townsman meets the countryman in much this way; the endless theme of country versus city usually deflates each. If remote from Xenophon's adventures and Plato's colloquies, this comic tolerance breathes at least a like naturalness.

To turn at last to the philosophers is daunting, and space is short even by the summary standard of these lectures. If Plato took one step of huger import than his many others, it was to have closed the split between *phusis* and *nomos,* nature and convention, which had come down to him from the fifth century. By *phusis* was meant the alien or impersonal working of nature, seemingly heedless of Greek standards, which had emerged to the inquiry of travelers and sophists. In Herodotus, Greeks at the Court of Darius are shocked to learn that Indians eat their dead parents, while the Indians are as pained that the Greeks burn theirs—at which Herodotus tolerantly observes that, as Pindar said, *nomos* is king.[15] When in Thucydides the besieged Melians express hope that the gods will help them, an Athenian general coldly replies: "In our opinion, the gods presumptively and mankind demonstrably hold power through natural compulsion."[16] Socrates was accused of substituting new gods—in effect, natural forces—for the old and is so represented in Aristophanes' *Clouds*. *Phusis* meant a world without gods. *Nomos* meant the received standards and pieties, which in the light of this contrast looked frail and provincial, a legacy from ages that had innocently failed to grasp, as one of Euripides' characters puts it, the conditions on which life is held. The early dialogues slowly move toward Plato's solution, which is elaborated in the *Republic*: namely, that nature itself is the source of human standards. The primacy of the mind, its support by emotion, and their joint control over appetite—an interworking that he calls justice and that he carries over from the individual to the state—represent no artificial or merely inherited system of values, but rather comprise the only means of happiness and order. Since violence to these relations necessarily produces disorder, they must be thought of as naturally implanted, the true pattern of our human nature. The consequences of this view are virtually limitless. It enthrones order at the center of things and makes the mind's task one of discerning it by dialectic, with entire confidence that what the mind perceives will not contradict but further clarify the regnant scheme. It closes the breach between animate and inanimate nature, because each will be seen to take its due place in the mighty system. Its universe is formed and limited, not chaotic and infinite; all parts of nature have their identifying shape and function, and nothing happens at random. In sum, it gives the assurance which the questing fifth-century mind increasingly lacked, that the seemingly infinite variety of the world is not in fact wild and ungoverned but open to understanding and hence to control. Control would in effect be simply the recognition and following of natural laws that exist in any case.

It is notoriously uncertain how far Socrates is to be read in these ideas; certainly he is not to be found in the elaborations of them that look to fourth-century conditions and controversies. For example, Aristophanes' late *Ecclesiazousae,* produced in 392, lampoons the community of women and children that Plato espouses in the *Republic,* probably of about 388;[17] the idea seems to have circulated in the shaken years after the war. Yet Socrates was all-important, not only personally to Plato in his early maturity, when his teacher's trial and death turned him from the political expectations of his upbringing to quite another kind of life,[18] but in Socrates' unwavering certainty, for all his professed ignorance, that truth and order existed if he could only find them. This certainty appears in the steady search of his questioning, and also in the credence with which he received the Delphic reply that, ignorant as he believed himself to be, he was the wisest of living men—evidently then by reason of his faith and search. It appears further in his obedience to an inner voice, his *daimonion,* which never told him what he should do but often what he should not.[19] Socrates' conviction that lives are intended to follow some scheme, which therefore must be rooted in nature, seems to have left Plato with the task of working out the implications and of trying to define more positively what this reality is that can thus command allegiance. Or so the relationship appears through his eyes; the actual Socrates is elusive except in his huge influence. Plato's path of elucidation was via the consequences of accepted standards. By analyzing any separate virtue such as courage or self-control, he could show it to be inconsistent or meaningless if taken by itself, hence that unless it was to be rejected it must derive authority from some wider scheme. The early so-called aporistic dialogues end in uncertainty because the isolated topic remains thus unclear and a larger relationship is not yet visible. In the longer early-middle dialogues, the *Gorgias* and *Protagoras,* going norms of success and routes to it in rhetoric and politics are attacked by like methods, with the now growing implication that these, unlike the admitted virtues treated earlier, represent corruptions of the true order, which accordingly comes nearer being defined. Through this long process Socrates' faith that some ways of behaving must be righter than others persists undoubted, and the eventual solution of the *Republic* is derivatively his, if not his in detail. Other strands have meanwhile appeared which are likewise woven into the *Republic*. If a greater scheme exists, it may be expected to govern more than one lifetime—hence the doctrine of recollection from other existences which shows in the *Meno*, also the visions of the afterlife of the *Gorgias, Phaedo,* and *Republic*. If, further, the mind is thus to rise to the truth, it must do so by some kind of flight or ascent, and in the *Symposium* love, joint offspring of poverty and riches, guides the winging soul from what it lacks to what it seeks.[20] This flight recalls the soul's emergence in the *Republic* from the shadowy and flickering cave of appearances to the light of truth, and the elaborate analogy that, as the sun allows the eyes to see, so truth allows the mind.[21] Though other dialogues are more vivid, more dramatic, and more brilliantly lit by grace and humor and feeling, and though Socrates seems more at home in them, the *Republic* is their logical summation.

The result is characteristically Greek in asserting external correlatives and sanctions to what we incline to call subjective or at least mental processes. Just as the Greek gods, variable though they may have been in cult, corporately comprise an analysis of the world—Athena as mind, Apollo as random and unpredictable illumination, Aphrodite as sexuality, Dionysus as change and excitement, Artemis as untouchedness, Hera as settlement and marriage, Zeus as order dominant over all—so the Platonic forms exist in their own right, lucent and eternal above any transitory human participation in them. Plato might not have approved this comparison, since the inherited figures of the gods were to him too anthropomorphic, too morally unclear, too logically undefined, to embody reality; yet they had long seemed to do so and to most Greeks still did; they were essences of life, by contemplation of which any individual life took on meaning and substance. The Platonic forms—also called ideas, though in a sense quite opposite to our subjective use of the word—thus served for him a double purpose. They were both analytical and, if one may use the term, essential: that is, they prescribed an order behind the confusions of appearance and they declared that order to be the only firm reality. To this view the important thing about a human being was not the accidents of parents, place of birth, circumstances of upbringing, stature, looks, temperament—in short, the many details that mark individuality. The important thing was his participation in an order greater than himself which endowed him with its more permanent being. The paradox is often noted that Socrates, whose round build and upturned nose could seem laughably unique and whose death marked him off from other men, fathered a doctrine that denied uniqueness. Alcibiades in the *Symposium* compared him to images of Silenus that on being opened prove to contain figures of gods;[22] the inside comes near being the denial of the outside.

After the founding of the Academy in 388, for which the *Republic* apparently served as a kind of charter,[23] the dialogues become more professorial, as Plato tries to work out the theory of forms among colleagues and pupils. This is hardly the place to pursue the complex effort, which involved, in the *Theaetetus,* epistemological questions of how the Heraclitan flux of appearance may be pierced and reliable knowledge achieved; in the *Parmenides,* problems of classification into groups and species; in the *Timaeus,* cosmological questions of the origin of the world by an act of the primal demiurge; in the *Philebus,* difficult logical questions about criteria of conduct. Though Plato's position doubtless changed in details as he faced these and other questions in the more workaday, less visionary setting of the Academy—the late *Laws,* for example, sharply revise the *Republic*—the temper of his mind seems strangely constant. His authoritarian tendency, his rejection of democracy—the democracy under which Socrates had been put to death—and his desire for trained rulers, all of which are often criticized today, seem secondary, as does his attack on poetry. He was first of all the spokesman for the new conceptuality that with pain and effort was replacing the old half-sensate reliance on myth; as such, he went much farther than Thucydides or his contemporaries in working out what must be stated of a world in which thought may be relied on. Like most Greeks he no doubt underrated the size and age of the world, and hence was relatively blind to the varieties of life and social order that might be expected to come into being—in this respect one may prefer Herodotus's fresh curiosity. He could not conceive of life without thought, thought without order, or (since we are in the world, hence help describe it) the world itself without structure and scheme. That he went one step farther reflects a Greek faith: he believed the beauty and dignity of thought to be so great as presumptively to share in the purpose of things. The gods themselves, by specifying spheres and planes of human life, let these partake of their pure being. Like the poets, Plato did not imagine that the best of life could be accidental, and though he spurned what he saw as the shadows of impression, he attributed absolute being to the bright structures of what he deemed sure knowledge.

Let us pause briefly to look back. The classic which emerged complete in Sophocles drew from legend, myth, and folktale because these in turn had elicited from the tangle of nature and history what seemed to be guiding clarifications. If the early stories flashed with the colors of life, these were not chaotic colors; they only brightened and made real the underlying analysis—formed a bridge, as it were, from the world of impression to the world of understanding. Thus stated, such duality between impression and idea is of course untrue of the first period; people saw the world as one and never doubted that the play of sense was compatible with comprehension—was in fact necessary to it. Yet the duality is worth stressing not only because the two sides later flew apart, but also because it helps describe the Greek bent of mind. If the purpose of the early stories was at bottom to clarify an otherwise chaotic world, this bent of mind was natively intellectual. The journeys of Odysseus, though they seem real and apparently move through actual places, are in substance analytical of experience; he sees not only different but representative people and places, and he returns with something like full knowledge of what life affords. This aim toward clarification is crucial; the early Greeks were evidently so sure of the world that they saw and touched that they could take it for granted as interesting and delightful; what was more gripping, because more elusive, was its laws and meanings. The direction of their thought was thus from the world toward idea, not the reverse; they wanted to simplify and to understand—not, to repeat, because they did not know or love the visible world, but because they sought more. The Sophoclean classic is the final issue of this long desire; by elimination and emphasis, it distills calmly illustrative shapes from the moil of circumstance and lifts accident into meaning, confusion into form. The classic as thus created seeks the generic in the unique, the illustrative in the passing, the norm in the mysterious—not because it is insensitive to the color of the world, but because it assumes this color to contain and even point to comprehensible meanings. The classic thus implies no pallor of feeling, is not achieved from insensitiveness or dull attraction to wooden truths. On the contrary, it is won from the fierce strain between pressing actuality and an equally stubborn drive toward meaning; it expresses, like a taut bow, an ultimate pressure between sensibility and mind.

It was this perilous balance, held momentarily in the great age, that came down unstrung to Plato. The emergence of the light Attic style that occupied us earlier shows pleasure and interest in the world as it is. That statement may not be quite fair or at least quite charitable; life has never been so easy (certainly it was not in the fourth century) that intelligent acceptance of the level light of every day lacks a tone of victory. But Socrates' single-minded life and heroic death showed to Plato a new dimension of the old heroism. His explanation of what he saw in Socrates—and also in the intellectuality of the sophists, misdirected though he thought it was—by older standards involved a shocking breach between truth and appearance. The earlier faith in the senses as at least guides to truth would never be so sure again, and with its loss some light left antiquity. Yet the change was inevitable; as we saw in Euripides and Thucydides, the old partnership between mind and impression was already partly broken, and to them and others the possibility that events might be explicable by pure idea had an almost hypnotic attraction. By crossing the bridge and taking his stand firmly on the other side, Plato—if the argument here is at all correct—kept faith with the main instinct of Greek thought. He wanted life to be intelligible; more, he wanted for it the dignity of participating in a great and permanent scheme. Pindar's victors had confirmed in the present the example of demigods, and Aeschylus's characters had made clear the divine teaching in history. If a man's actions lacked for Plato this quasi-personal guidance by gods and heroes, they could take reality from final forms—including the form of the good itself[24]—which to him were still nobler than the gods. In this view, the quiet of the previously quoted opening of the *Republic* shows a dailyness that does not lack hold on permanence. The term *l'esprit géométrique*[25] has been used for a mid-seventeenth-century bareness that eschewed grandeur for cogency, and the words come to mind to describe, if not the highest flights of the dialogues, at least their common setting. Actual people, not legendary heroes, pursue trains of thought and, in the case of Socrates, perform final actions that verge toward the great norms. These lie at the edge of the daily, which, though in another light it can seem illusory and full of shadow and danger, still keeps access to bright permanence.

It was said that Plato's closing of the split between *phusis* and *nomos* was his most far-reaching act, as in sheer length of influence it clearly was. Greek philosophy was increasingly engrafted onto Christianity, and if the terms and methods of their closest union in the late Middle Ages were Aristotelian, yet Aristotle began as a Platonist and in important ways remained one. He was a member of the Academy from his twentieth to his fortieth year, until Plato's death in 348; history can hardly show a more extraordinary apprenticeship, or at least so long an apprenticeship that proved not to cramp the younger man's quite different temperament. Using fragments of Aristotle's lost early works, the late Werner Jaeger traced his evolution from the Academy to the Lyceum,[26] and showed that the centuries-old impression of him as born complete like Athena simply reflects the fact that the full system of his extant works derives from his last years. His final rationalism far outstripped his teacher's. Plato in the *Timaeus* had posited a vagrant passivity in matter[27]—what he calls *ananke,* necessity—that blurs the imprint of the primal artificer, hence leaves the world an imperfect copy of the divine plan. This dualism in Plato between mind and matter is obviously not complete; if it had been, nature would not have exhibited the guiding order that he chiefly sought. Yet the flaw was real enough to make the appetites rebellious, to fill life with the shadows of false appearance, and to spur the soul's upward flight toward truth. Plato's struggle against the politics that had caused the death of Socrates, and more fundamentally against the color and emotion of popular and poetic thought, gave him a tone of exhortation; the early dialogues commonly begin with an incitement to the good life, and at Syracuse he tried seriously though unsuccessfully to train and guide the young tyrant Dionysius II. But neither temperament nor the logic of his system gave Aristotle this redemptive purpose. His position toward Plato somewhat resembles that of Sophocles toward Aeschylus; the younger men saw themselves not as innovators but as continuators, free to tighten and clarify the creative forms that their volcanic predecessors had cast up. Aristotle accordingly discarded the recalcitrant and irrational element in things that in Plato slightly obscures the final forms. In the *Nicomachean Ethics* nothing clouds the possible working of free will; a rational man is quite able to make the choices on which virtue and happiness depend; nature does not impede—on the contrary, it commends—the orderly conduct of a life. If the old breach between *phusis* and *nomos* was closed in Plato, it was cemented tight in Aristotle.

The progressive infusion of this rational clarity into Christianity, complete in the Ptolemaic astronomy and the Thomism of the thirteenth century, shows the extent of Plato's victory. That the world seemed orderly for more than a millennium and a half was not least his doing. It is true that Aristotle retreated from Plato's vision of the ideal forms to find order in the common working of nature. Of his four causes[28]—the material, the efficient, the formal, and the final

—the last two are dominant, and every part of nature strives to fulfill its implanted function. By teleology the oak is implicit in the acorn; all material things, inanimate and animate, take their due place in a great chain of being. Since mind holds the highest place in the chain, and since mankind finds its identifying attribute in mind, human happiness to Aristotle lies in contemplation. "If happiness be activity in accordance with virtue," he writes in the tenth book of the *Nicomachean Ethics*,[29] "it is reasonable that it be in accordance with the highest virtue, and this would belong to that which is best in us. Be this mind or something else which naturally rules and directs and has comprehension of things beautiful and divine—be it itself divine or the divinest of our attributes—its activity through its native virtue will be perfect happiness." Here is the fulfillment, without mist or flaw, of a beautifully intelligible world. Now Alfred North Whitehead called the nascent science of the Renaissance anti-rational,[30] in the sense that its empiricism precisely rejected the marvelous edifice of Aristotelian reason. In tracing by experiment or experience how things actually take place, Galileo and Machiavelli preferred demonstrable truth, however disturbing, to doctrine, however consistent; with the result—when this empiricism was endlessly multiplied—that something like the old split between *phusis* and *nomos* has returned. The world is no longer a closed system crowned by human intelligence. Thus if, as suggested, the fourth century has somewhat lost its grip on us, the reason seems double: we take for granted its daily clarities but doubt its final clarifications. The danger of circumstance and the impassive distance of the gods in the *Oedipus Tyrannus* can seem truer to us than the orderliness of Aristotle's *Ethics,* and in Plato Socrates' heroic choice can outweigh the ideal forms. Investigation in a thousand fields has brought back on a huge scale the very sense of nature's vagaries that chilled the confidence of the fifth century and prompted Plato's passionate search for a solution.

These lectures accordingly end in a paradox. Though that part of Plato and Aristotle which looked to reasoned analysis and defined concept has gone on to untold victories, yet older elements of Greek thought—elements that they denied and hoped to supplant—have lost none of their authority. For if (to invoke the biggest) our solar system lies only at the edge of the unimaginable galaxy of the Milky Way, which in turn gives on still more unimaginable galaxies beyond, any faith in our human senses involves a kind of heroism. The Homeric heroism with which we started seemed precisely to rest on trust in the senses; however briefly the heroes lived, they never doubted the sparkle of the world's invitation. If they saw beyond them, not distant galaxies, but timeless gods unchanging above the beach and plain of Troy, the disparity was in effect as large. Yet, strange to relate, it did not daunt either the heroes or Homer and his listeners, who saw in the gods' bright eternity some kinship with their own brief world. As mathematicians attribute a kind of eternity—less of duration than of form and idea—to perfect theorems, so mountains and rivers, ships and waves, fields and animals, men and gods, keep in Homer their special timelessness. We may not ascribe this impression to our distance from Homer; his lucidities were as clear to the ancients. Thus our first conclusion is that clarity of response is fundamental. Plato and Aristotle wanted a conceptual clarity and much in our civilization follows from their choice, but to Homer this clarity of the mind came second to the clarity of the senses. He was not, as we have seen, uninterested in idea; though he lacked terminology for Odysseus as a philosopher, the famous travels of the *Odyssey* comprise in fact an analysis of the outflung world (Aeolus's winds, the Laestrygonians' long daylight, the terrors of Scylla and Charybdis, the Sun's cloud-like cattle), of society (the rude Cyclops and the refined Phaeacians), and of inner states (the slack Lotuseaters, Circe's sexual and the Sirens' intellectual realms, the illustrative dead, Calypso's eternity in nature). In victoriously uniting life as potentiality and movement with life as attainment and rest, Odysseus is himself as illustrative as anything that he saw. Achilles as clearly shows another destiny: of doing rather than seeing, or at least of illumination entangled in doing and bought from its stress—the sudden, blazing knowledge of youth rather than the wider and slower knowledge of later life. But these and other clarifications of Homer are not hurried, not isolated as idea from events and impressions as if these were secondary, not wrenched from experience but freshly and, as it were, inevitably cast up by it. Heroism then seems born of clear feeling, itself the child of clear impression. Granted that Homer saw or thought that he saw a fresh world crowned (not at all spoiled) by men's inventions, yet life's freshness is perpetually renewed, and response to it is our first faith.

The classic, as we have seen, is the calm of tension, the

poise of the bow fully stretched. The opposed forces may be variously conceived, though in some difficult final sense each side is doubtless one. Intellectually conceived, Sophocles' *Oedipus Tyrannus* expresses the farthest possible condensation of impression into form. Aeschylus and Pindar had moved beyond Homer in this direction; the world to them was full of hints and analogies which complexly pointed to underlying laws—sibylline leaves, as it were, cryptic and multitudinous—but their pre-classic vitality did not quite unite their search for meaning with their response to the play and color of the world. Aeschylus's aquiline language soars to evoke Xerxes' enormous army and the peoples that Prometheus sees from his crag, and Pindar leaps from present to legendary victories; yet beneath all their variegation speaks in Aeschylus the divine teaching through history, in Pindar the real, though lesser, likeness of present feats to those of the demigods. Only Sophocles achieves the classic balance between sensibility and idea. Methodologically conceived, the union renounces width for depth: renounces, that is, the sheer extension in time and space of the Homeric epics and Aeschylean trilogies, in favor of illustrative moments when destinies stand clear. In this act of compression is doubtless some triumph of idea; as we saw, the chiseled contrast between the claims of the state and those of the family in the *Antigone,* between the prophet's physical and the king's mental blindness in the *Oedipus,* subtly reflects the new intellectuality of the later fifth century. Yet Sophocles did not think by concepts but by situations, and the marvel of the classic as seen in him is its ability, while still heeding the senses, to discern their guiding norms. Conceived as an act of faith, this distil-

lation continues to share Homer's response to the brightness
of the world but goes a step farther. It lifts stable shapes from
the evanescent variety of things and makes of their illustra-
tiveness a compressed testimony about the world. *Bíos biós,*
said Heraclitus in a famous pun—life is a bow.[31] Without the
bow of perception the string of mind has nothing to com-
press, but without the string of mind the sensibilities hang
limp and unrecognized. Since the world changes and with it
our sensibilities, thought too must change. Hence the classic
as the climax of this tense harmony of bow and bowstring is
by nature transient, forever needing recreation. Youth and
promise contain freshness of feeling even when it is incom-
pletely grasped. But if with further knowledge the sensibilities grow stiff, the bowstring draws on triteness. The classic
as the bow at the full expresses faith in a perpetually endan-
gered comprehension.

The revolution by which conceptual thinking replaced the
old reliance on myth necessarily shook the brief balance of
the great age. As a cause of change, this intellectual revolution far outweighs even the strain of the twenty-seven-year
war. We saw in Euripides and Thucydides the first steps of
the change—deeply affecting steps, in that both men were
sufficiently drawn to the old synoptic ways of seeing things
brilliantly to expound norms and classes of experience, yet
with an underlying sense that these jarred harshly with ordinary life. The very triumphs of the great age had so enlarged
the world that any events, whether of the theater or of the
actual war, lacked some footing when considered simply as
parts of Greek experience; they implied some wider, more
inclusive natural order that they might seem to confirm or

illustrate. Both men subtly assume this order without defining it, and their sense of regnant universals adds to the poignancy of the blindly endured sufferings that they set forth. Aristotle called Euripides the most tragic of the playwrights, in part at least because his characters seem somehow lost, intellectually though many of them talk. Thucydides wrote to clarify for future statesmen the scheme of the war, and thought that the Athenians might have won if they had avoided a few crucial errors; yet even to him some iron necessity seems to guide events, and its working belies his rational optimism. The conceptual advances of Euripides and Thucydides touched chiefly the surface, below which lay danger and irrationality. That Plato and Aristotle dispelled this underlying disorder (disorder from the point of view of human life and conduct) and set forth a morally comprehensible scheme in nature has been the burden of this last lecture. They did so for a society in which both the common things of life and the styles for expressing them were now fully accepted; it is a curious fact that ordinariness seems the precondition of theory, evidently because some exactitude of mind is common to both. Yet whether faith in reason or faith in the living example of Socrates more deeply prompted Plato is hard to guess. If at bottom he thought the two faiths one, as he doubtless did, the fact would reaffirm that interworking between sensibility and mind—between our bright impressions of the world and our wish to simplify and explain them—which is peculiarly Greek. Whether below the gods at Troy or below Plato's ideal forms or below the unimaginable galaxies, faith in the tension may not much differ.

NOTES

NOTES

Chapter One

1. Horace, *De Arte Poetica*; Longinus, *On the Sublime*; Quintilian, *Institutio Oratoria* X. It is agreed that *On the Sublime* was wrongly attributed by early editors to the third-century rhetorician Longinus; the familiar name is used for convenience. See the edition of W. Rhys Roberts (Cambridge, England, 1907), pp. 1–23.

2. vv. 466–73.

3. vv. 290–327.

4. A bibliography of Parry accompanies H. T. Levin's "Portrait of a Homeric Scholar," *Classical Journal,* XXXII (1937), 259–66.

5. C. M. Bowra in A. J. B. Wace and F. H. Stubbings, eds., *A Companion to Homer* (London, 1962), pp. 41–42.

6. *Homeric Hymn to Apollo* 172. The Phaeacian bard Demodocus is blind (*Od.* VIII 64). Similarly the divine smith Hephaestus is lame. Early society seems to have made use of men with impaired faculties.

7. *On the Sublime* 9.13.

8. *Od.* XI 367–68; XVII 518–21.

9. *Od.* VIII 471–83; XXII 330–77.

10. *Il.* XI 765–82.

11. A. B. Lord describes the lonely self-instruction of young Jugoslav singers in *The Singer of Tales* (Cambridge, Mass., 1960), p. 21.

12. *Il.* XVI 34–35.

13. *Poetics* 4.1348b34, 8.1451a29, 23–24.1459a30–b16.

14. *Il.* VI 459–65; VII 299–302.

15. vv. 349–50.

16. *Il.* XIV 85–87.

17. XVI 83–96.

18. *Il.* XXII 359–60.

19. *Il.* IX 410–16.

20. *Il.* XX 115–28.

21. *Od.* XXIV 36–62.

22. *Ibid.,* 93–97.

23. *Ibid.,* 192–98.

24. W. Schadewaldt, *Von Homers Welt und Werk,* 2d ed. (Stuttgart, 1951), pp. 155–202. C. H. Whitman, *Homer and the Heroic Tradition* (Cambridge, Mass., 1958), pp. 269–70.

25. *Isth.* 8.62–66.

26. *Il.* XXII 147–56.

27. *Od.* I 58; V 306–12.

28. *Od.* IX 224–28; X 169–74.

29. *Od.* V 203–24.

30. *Ibid.,* 63–95.

31. *Od.* XI 119–37.

32. *Od.* XII 403–19; XXII 481–82.

33. *Od.* V 490.

34. E. Vermeule, *Greece in the Bronze Age* (Chicago, 1964), pp. 138, 172. *Od.* XIII 103–12.

35. A. Malraux, *Les Voix de Silence* (Paris, 1956), pp. 72–78, 233.

36. A. Heidel, *The Gilgamesh Epic and Old Testament Parallels* (Chicago, 1946), Tables VII and XII.

37. *Od.* X 84–85.

38. *Od.* IX 106–15; VIII 557–63.

39. *Od.* XII 184–91.

40. *Od.* VIII 447–48.

41. *Od.* XXIII 183–204.

42. *Od.* XXI 128–29.

Chapter Two

1. *Od.* VI 162–63; *Il.* IV 481–89.

2. V 78.

3. Scholium on v. 94, Murray's Oxford text, p. 150.

4. *Ag.* 40–59.

5. *Ag.* 104–59.

6. *Ag.* 176–83.

7. *Ag.* 551–74.

8. *Ag.* 395.

9. *Ag.* 773–81.

10. *Ag.* 908–13.

11. *Ag.* 1331–34.

12. I 17.

13. *Ag.* 1355, 1633; *Cho.* 973.

14. *Cho.* 523–39.

15. *Cho.* 269–84.

16. *Cho.* 900–902.

17. *Eum.* 212.

18. *Eum.* 213–24.

19. *Eum.* 40–87, 235–43, 614–73, 734–73.

20. *Eum.* 734–41.

21. *Eum.* 937–1020.

22. *Ag.* 176–78, 250–51, 1564; *Cho.* 313.

23. *Cho.* 247.

24. *Ag.* 367, 1343.

25. *Ag.* 358, 1116, 1382; *Cho.* 999–1000; *Eum.* 306.

26. *Ag.* 22, 508, 900, 1577.

27. Diels-Kranz, *Die Vorsokratiker*, 6th ed. (Berlin, 1951), I, frs. 1, 17, 41, 50, 70, 104.

28. *O.* 1.1–6.   29. *O.* 11.1–6; *N.* 4.1–5.

30. *O.* 1.81–84, 87.   31. *P.* 10.27; *N.* 6.1–7.

32. *Vorsokratiker*, I, frs. 2, 8, 10, 30, 31, 36, 60, 76.

33. *Ibid.*, fr. 119.

34. *Poetics* 16.1455a18, 18.1456a27, 26.1462b3.

35. Similarity to the *Hippolytus* of 428 b.c. in use of the argument from likelihood (*O.T.* 583–615; *Hipp.* 983–1020); similarity to the *Trachiniae*, usually dated in the 430's, in use of a second messenger who confronts the first (*O.T.* 1123–85; *Trach.* 402–96); possible repetition of v. 629 in *Acharnians* of 425 b.c. (v. 27).

36. *Poetics* 9.1451b5.   37. *O.T.* 436.

38. *O.T.* 1060–61.

Chapter Three

1. In V 26.5 he says that he was of an age to have followed the whole course of the war—a statement that seems to refute the suspicion that he might have been either too young at the outset or too old at the end. But he could not have imagined himself too old at the end, when he was in the full flow of his writing; hence seems tacitly to admit that he was young at the start but not so young as to have failed to follow events closely.

2. I 99.3.

3. *Pericles* 6.

4. See especially the opening of *On Ancient Medicine,* also W. H. S. Jones, *Hippocrates* (Loeb Classical Library, New York, 1923), Vol. I, Introduction, pp. xiv–xxi, lii–lv.

5. On Hippodamus, see Pauly-Wissowa-Kroll, *Realencyclopedie,* XVI, 1731–33; on Meton, *ibid.,* XXX, 1458–63; on Polyclitus, *ibid.,* XLII, 1711–12.

6. *Vorsokratiker*, II, fr. 4.   7. *Hipp.* 375–87.

8. *Medea* 1078–80.   9. *Apology* 25e; *Protagoras* 352c.

10. For example, the young Macaria of the *Heracleidae* (474 ff.) and Meneceus of the *Phoenissae* (977 ff.).

11. *Hipp.* 433–81.   12. *Hipp.* 1441.

13. *Medea* 824–45.   14. *Ba.* 810 ff.

15. *Ba.* 425–32.   16. V 26.5.

17. *The Idea of History* (Oxford, 1946).

18. I 22.4.   19. III 82.2–4.

20. VII 28.3.

21. II 40.1.

22. II 65.

23. IV 17–20.

24. I 22.4.

25. *Protagoras* 319a.

26. II 48.3 echoes the prognostic purpose of the *History* expressed in I 22.4. See C. N. Cochrane, *Thucydides and the Science of History* (Oxford, 1929).

27. I 76.2.

28. II 36–41.

29. II 62.

30. II 64.

31. I 144.

32. VI 24.3.

33. I 76.2; V 86–113.

34. VII 86.5; II 65.11; VI 15.

35. II 60.6.

36. IV 21.

Chapter Four

1. *Knights* 174. Cf. 1088–89, 1303. Thuc. VI 32.

2. Thuc. II 64.3–4.

3. *Apology* 26d–e.

4. *Birds* 923 ff.

5. *Republic* VIII 557d.

6. Thuc. II 38.1, 40.1.

7. Polybius IV 21.

8. *Anabasis* IV 5.15–36.

9. *Achar.* 665–75; *Peace* 1161–69.

10. *Anabasis* II 6.

11. *Protagoras* 314d–316a.

12. Athenaeus XIII 603e–604d. A. von Blumenthal, *Ion Von Chios* (Stuttgart, 1939), p. 11.

13. A. Meineke, *Fragmenta Comicorum Graecorum* (Berlin, 1839), I, 374–90; III, 452, 454, 457, 484, 490, 493, 506, 508, 509, 519. The statement of Suidas that Alexis was Menander's uncle has been doubted.

14. H. Lloyd-Jones, *Menandri Dyscolus* (Oxford, 1960), pp. v, 3.

15. Herod. III 38.

16. Thuc. V 105.2.

17. A. E. Taylor, *Plato,* 3d ed. (London, 1929), p. 6.

18. *Seventh Epistle* 324c–326b.

19. *Apology* 21a, 40a–c.

20. *Symposium* 203b ff.

21. *Republic* VII 514a–518c, VI 507d–509c.

22. *Symposium* 215a–b.

23. A. E. Taylor, *Plato,* 3d ed., p. 6.

24. *Republic* VI 507a–b; *Seventh Letter* 342b–344c.

25. G. N. Clark, *The Seventeenth Century* (Oxford, 1929), p. 335.

26. *Aristoteles* (Berlin, 1922).

27. *Timaeus* 48a.

28. *Physics* II 3.

29. X 7.1177a12–17.

30. *Science and the Modern World* (New York, 1941), p. 12.

31. *Vorsokratiker,* I, fr. 48.